ALIENS

GOD

═══ **AND THE** ═══

BIBLE

4880 Lower Valley Road • Atglen, PA 19310

A THEOLOGICAL SPECULATIVE STUDY OF THE BIBLE'S ALIEN MYSTERIES

THE REV. DR. JOEL CURTIS GRAVES

Designed by Danielle D. Farmer
Cover design by Matthew Goodman

Scripture taken from the HOLY BIBLE: NEW INTERNATIONAL VERSION®. Copyright © 1973, 1978, 1984 by International Bible Society. Used by permission of Zondervan Publishing House. All rights reserved. The "NIV" and "New International Version" trademarks are registered in the United States Patent and Trademark Office by International Bible Society. Use of either trademark requires the permission of the International Bible Society.

Type set in Praetorian/Trajan Pro/Nexus Mix/ITC Officina Sans

ISBN: 978-0-7643-5356-7
Printed in the United States of America

Published by Schiffer Publishing, Ltd.
4880 Lower Valley Road
Atglen, PA 19310
Phone: (610) 593-1777; Fax: (610) 593-2002
E-mail: Info@schifferbooks.com
Web: www.schifferbooks.com

For our complete selection of fine books on this and related subjects, please visit our website at www.schifferbooks.com. You may also write for a free catalog.

Schiffer Publishing's titles are available at special discounts for bulk purchases for sales promotions or premiums. Special editions, including personalized covers, corporate imprints, and excerpts, can be created in large quantities for special needs. For more information, contact the publisher.

We are always looking for people to write books on new and related subjects. If you have an idea for a book, please contact us at proposals@schifferbooks.com.

Portrait of an alien 3D rendering. Black background © sarah5
Arc de Triomphe the parisian monument of the second world war © Zoltan Kiraly
Legendary Ark of the Covenant from the Bible © jgroup
CENTRAL AFRICAN REPUBLIC - NOVEMBER 2 2008: The white person the tourist and women from a tribe of pygmies of Bakf in the forest. Dzanga-Sangha Forest Reserve Central African Republic Nov. 2 2008 © SURZ
Winged angel gravestone back view in black and white © kasha_malasha

To my wife, children, and grandchildren.
To all kids who ask hard Bible questions
that adults struggle to answer.
To all theologians who have struggled
with these questions since the beginning.
And to all scientists who fearlessly admit
they are really searching for God.

Science can discover the fingerprints of God, which is why the Bible begins with the Creation event.

—by the Rev. Dr. Joel Curtis Graves
with nod to Moses Maimonides
(1135-1204), and his *Guide for the Perplexed* (1191)

To raise new questions, new possibilities,
to regard old problems from a new angle,
requires creative imagination
and marks real advance in science.

—Albert Einstein

The heavens declare the glory of God;
the skies proclaim the work of his hands.

—King David, Psalm 19:1

CONTENTS

FOREWORD

BY BISHOP DAVID JOHN BENA

Americans have a thing for roller coasters. We have more per capita than any other nation in the world. In *Aliens, God, and the Bible: A Theological Speculative Study of the Bible's Alien Mysteries*, the Reverend Doctor Joel Graves takes us on a roller coaster ride like no other. Buckle your seatbelt and enjoy this theological thriller. Joel has put together what may become a classic in the Christian speculative theology genre.

As I read chapter after chapter, my brain expanded to its breaking point while trying to tie it all together. The author moves deeply into speculative and scientific theology without ever leaving biblical orthodoxy. You will read about the sensational Spaceship of Revelation and then backtrack into Genesis as Joel explains why things happened: the Fall of Adam, Satan and the cosmic battle, God's intervention through the salvific work of Jesus, all in the context of planet Earth as a tiny speck in the universe deeply loved by God.

In this swashbuckling book, he ties the Bible together end to end. You name it, it's in there: the nature of the universe and how it works scientifically, the problem with evolution, the Neanderthal, Sasquatch, Jesus and his decent to planet Earth, even the presence of space aliens and where they come from.

In this exciting thrill-packed book, Joel works to bridge the bible-science gap. Perhaps someday, *Aliens, God, and the Bible* will be a seminary textbook for the subject of Speculative Theology. Are you ready for the ride of your life?

Bishop Bena is a retired US Air Force chaplain, bishop in the Anglican Church in North America (ACNA) and the Convocations of Anglicans in North America (CANA). He is the author of *In The Crucible, Vols 1–3*, and *Your Faith: Memorial, Memory or Miracle?*

PREFACE

If you do not care for contemplations about what is happening or not happening in the world, the future, and the Bible, put this book down right now and run away. Within these pages I will talk frankly about what the Bible says, what it does mean in some places, and what it *might* mean in others—especially in the near future. I call it Speculative Theology based on mysteries, facts, clues, and allusions found in the world, but especially in the Bible.

Speculative Theology is "okay" occasionally, if you do not spend all of your time there and miss the truly important message. I think of speculation as *wonder* in question form: *I wonder what . . . I wonder if . . .* or, *I wonder what was really going on there . . .* So every now and then, when speculation begins to inform our search for knowledge and truth, we have nothing to lose but our ignorance.

Albert Einstein once said, "The important thing is not to stop questioning. Curiosity has its own reason for existing. One cannot help but be in awe when he contemplates the mysteries of eternity, of life, of the marvelous structure of reality. It is enough if one tries merely to comprehend a little of this mystery every day. Never lose a holy curiosity."

I come by my wonder of God naturally. I was twelve. In the Anglican Church, Confirmation is a big deal. Most young adults are baptized as infants, and at Confirmation they proclaim their faith in Christ as the bishop lays hands on them to receive the Holy Spirit (*confirming* the promises made by sponsors at baptism). Our minister solemnly instructed candidates to read the Bible. After school once a week, I met with him and quickly learned that he did not appreciate me asking too many questions. "Where did Cain get his wife?" I smile to remember his flustered responses and gentle rebukes.

I call it a God-given curiosity.

"In the beginning, God . . ."

At the same time, we lived on a small farm in central California near the coast. One day while hoeing weeds in the garden, I stopped and looked up at the steep hill behind the house. The late summer long, dry, yellow grasses waving in the afternoon breeze touched the profound blue, and I marveled in appreciation and delight.

Suddenly a thought entered my head, based on my reading of Genesis 1:1, *"In the beginning God created the heavens and the earth,"* and what I was learning in Confirmation class. If there was *absolutely nothing* in the beginning, nothing at all—no dimensions, no universes, not even space itself—N O T H I N G—then where did God come from? How is it that God exists at all, and is then powerful enough to create all that we know and understand?

Throughout this book I refer to God in the masculine because King David described him as *father to the fatherless* (Psalm 68:5), and Jesus called him *Father* (John 10:30), although I am aware that God is probably genderless, as we understand gender.

The Bible. I believe the whole thing—every word—inerrant, also referred to as God's *Word* to humankind. *"The Word of God is living and active . . ."* (Hebrews 4:12). Not in a fundamentalist sort of way: I am willing to discuss, speculate, and debate what some things might mean or do not mean without being fearfully rigid and unimaginative. Asking questions about the Bible does not challenge or threaten my faith, because the foundation is firm. If you do not feel like your own foundation is particularly firm, I hope this book will cause you to grow in your knowledge of the Bible and relationship with God, both of which will be of great benefit to you in this life.

Sometimes passages seem awry or difficult, when it might be that we do not have enough information or facts to understand what was going on with the author, the culture, the writing, or why. There will always be ideas and concepts we cannot completely fathom and many things we will not fully grasp. And for the questions without answers—*Where did God come from?*—all we can do is wait.

Some people's biblical and religious beliefs are deeply entrenched, long-held, passed down through the ages and supported by deep emotional underpinnings. With these folks, some of my speculations might be upsetting or ardently avoided. However, I believe the Bible is full of flavor, and I am keen to share it like a rich cup of coffee from freshly roasted beans. If you do not agree on some point (preferring tea!), that is to be expected—few agree on everything. Between these pages and your ears, I am going to stretch your imagination—a lot. I will simply lay out the facts and ideas, give you my take on the matter, make a few pointed suggestions along the way, and let you decide for yourself what is going on. And at the end, I will talk about how speculation leads to preparation.

Besides, when the Bible says something like this, it feeds my imagination and makes me wonder, *"What no eye has seen, what no ear has heard, and what no human mind has conceived—the things God has prepared for those who love him"* (The Apostle Paul paraphrasing Isaiah 64:4 in his first letter to the church he started in Corinth, chapter 2, verse 9, abbreviated 1 Corinthians 2:9 or 1 Cor 2:9).

"What no human mind has conceived . . ."—you know I take this as a personal challenge. Meanwhile, I invite you to speculate with me, taking the challenge on as your own. I guarantee we will have fun and learn a lot.

Mark Twain wrote, "Most people are bothered by those passages in scripture which they cannot understand; but as for me, I always notice that the passages in scripture which trouble me most are those which I do understand."

I added this quote here as a reminder that while speculation is fun and stimulates our wonder and search for knowledge, we cannot let these ideas and questions derail or deflect simple obedience to God's Word. We do not want to be so speculatively-minded that we are of no earthly good.

I use the terms Satan and devil to describe the same personage. The word and name Satan means slanderer and adversary (*"for the accuser of our brethren has been thrown down, he who accuses them before our God day and night"* (Revelation 12:10 New American Standard (NAS); Zechariah 3:1), and *devil* literally means goat.

Unless otherwise noted, all scripture references are from the New International Version (NIV) of the Bible.

Throughout the book, I capitalize the word "Bible" to identify it as the Holy Bible of Judeo-Christian origins.

Although I belong to the Anglican Church in North America (ACNA), the thoughts and ideas in this book are my own and do not necessarily reflect Anglican doctrine, dogma, or theology. At the same time, I can assure you that nothing written here conflicts with the Creeds, the 39 Articles of Anglican Faith, or the orthodox teachings of the Church.

ACKNOWLEDGMENTS

I am indebted to my parents for fostering in me the desire to know God and ask questions about the things I did not understand. I am indebted to Bishop David Bena for his longtime friendship and editorial skills. The love of my life, Rena, has been patient with my writing, *and her children and grandchildren arise and call her Blessed; her husband also, and he praises her* (Proverbs 31:28). Thank you to Dinah Roseberry at Schiffer Publishing for seeing the value of this book and me as an author.

THE

CHAPTER ONE

SPACE
SHIP

ALL VISITING ALIENS NEED A SPACESHIP

What book about aliens would be complete without space travel? Did you know the Bible talks about a great cube-shaped spaceship coming to Earth?

In the *Star Trek* movie and television series, an alien race of cyborgs—the Borg Collective (half-humanoid, half-machine)—pilot a starship in the shape of a cube, approximately 3,000 meters to a side—almost two miles. Immense. Dwarfing the many Federation starships attacking it.

A CUBE SPACESHIP?

In Earth's atmosphere, flying objects need to be aerodynamic—sleek and smooth. A jet airliner flies through the air more efficiently than an upright piano. However, in space, an object can have almost any shape and still move freely—no air resistance. The International Space Station is a good example—lots of parts connected in various configurations while racing across the heavens at over 17,000 miles per hour (2,736 kmph), passing over us approximately sixteen times every day.

International Space Station. *Courtesy NASA.*

The Apostle John wrote, *"And I saw the holy city, New Jerusalem, coming down out of heaven from God."* (The Revelation of John, chapter 21, verse 2—abbreviated Rev 21:2—last book in the Bible).

What is this *New Jerusalem* object descending to Earth—from outer space—from God?

The angel explains to John that this great flying object is actually a city. A city? What else could the angel call it so John would understand? He might tell John it is a type of ship for traveling in the heavens, but even that could be confusing. John might ask, "Similar to a ship on the sea but it flies? A cube ship?" The great size would stretch his mind even further.

The angel could have called it a temple, a type of building. John was familiar with the Great Temple in Jerusalem. A flying temple would be an appropriate description when God is present. But by describing the New Jerusalem as a city tells John, and us, that people will gather there, live in community, enjoy an infrastructure, have a government with leadership, a purpose—and destinations.

Some controversy exists over the exact size.
The next scripture is a literal translation of the Greek:

And the city foursquare lies, and the length of it the same as moreover the width, also he measured the city with the reed, at STADIA twelve thousand: the length, and the breadth, and the height of it, equal are (Rev 21:16).

This version of the same verse is from the New Living Translation (NLT):

When he measured it, he found it was a square, as wide as it was long. In fact, its length and width and height were each 1,400 miles.

This passage is from the New American Standard Bible (NAS):

The city is laid out as a square, and its length is as great as the width; and he measured the city with the rod, 1,500 miles; its length and width and height are equal.

Did you notice the difference in size—1,400 miles and 1,500 miles? Remember, the Borg ship was two miles square.

How long is 12,000 stadia?

Biblical scholars debate the use of stadia, making it 1,400 miles (New Living Translation), and furlongs, making it 1,500 miles (New American Standard). No one is sure, because the precise specifications of these measurement standards in biblical times seem to be lost in antiquity. However, I showed you the literal Greek of the passage to emphasize that John meant to use the word *stadia*. So what is the problem?

The word stadia comes from the Latin *stadium*, based on the layout of a Roman coliseum—one-eighth of a Roman mile. Think of the movie *Ben-Hur* (1959) with chariots racing wildly around the track. As a resident and traveler of the Roman Empire, John would be familiar with Roman units of measure.

One stadia equals an eighth of a mile, so divide 12,000 stadia by eight to get 1,500 "Roman" miles. Now here is where the debate begins. How does a Roman mile of the first century measure up to an English statute mile of more recent times? The Roman mile is slightly shorter.

The word *mile* is of Latin origin for "thousand," and *passus* is Latin for "paces," so *mille passus* means "a thousand paces." As the Roman Legionaries marched along, they marked off one-mile increments every thousand paces. At the end of the day, they knew exactly how far they had walked since morning.

Therefore, to determine the distance of a Roman mile, we need to know the length of the basic pace. Roman scholars agreed that from the lifting of the heel of the left foot to the planting of the left heel again was a complete pace—two steps—approximately five feet. From that came the millarium. Every 1,000 paces, a millarium stone was placed (5,000 Roman feet), which in England became known as the *milestone.* I can imagine Roman soldiers marching along with someone acting as counter, if there were no milestones near the road to indicate previously measured distances.

Scholars determined that the Roman five-foot pace turned out to be 58 modern inches instead of our standard 60 inches. The difference between the Roman mile based on a 58-inch pace and our modern mile is 91.54 percent, making the ship 1,373 miles to a side.

However, evidence of the Roman system of measurement—the milestone—is still visible today. We can actually see and measure the Roman mile between ancient milestones at approximately 91.98 percent of the statue mile we are familiar with now, making each side of the ship 1,380 miles. Then which measurement do we use?

The measurement 1,373 miles is a good number, shorter than 1,380 by only 6.704 miles over this great distance. On the ground that equates to a seriously minor variation of only 4.25 thousandths (.00425) of an inch per mile. In this case, I am going to use the milestone calculation, because 1,380 is divisible by twelve, which turns out to be somewhat important.

What does this mean for our ship?

The New Jerusalem would actually be 1,380 statute miles (2,221 km) to a side, not 1,400 or 1,500 miles, as recorded in some Bible translations. The length, width, and height are each 1,380 miles—a great cube.

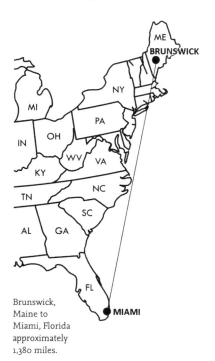

Brunswick, Maine to Miami, Florida approximately 1,380 miles.

How far is 1,380 miles?

Driving from Boston to Miami is 1,498 miles (2,410 km) along highways with typical twists and turns. If you lay out a straight line for one edge of the cube, the measurement would go—as the crow flies—from Brunswick, Maine, to Miami, Florida—essentially, *all of the East Coast.* (Brunswick lies between Augusta in the north and Portland in the south.)

Let's say this line is the bottom right or eastern side of the cube base. The northern edge would go from Brunswick, Maine, to Jamestown, North Dakota. Now go south 1,380 miles to reach the southern tip of Texas—south of Laredo into Mexico. This means the footprint of the cube would cover all of the United States east of central Texas.

New Jerusalem resting on Earth, covering much of the United States.

The planet Pluto. Box outline represents the New Jerusalem

The ship size is hard to grasp. One edge could go east from San Diego past Houston, just shy of Port Arthur, Texas, or heading north from San Diego to Regina, Saskatchewan, Canada. The cube base would cover most of the United States wherever it happened to land.

One side is 2,221 km: Paris to Istanbul—2,253 km, and Brussels to Moscow—2,253 km are just a little beyond that distance. Jerusalem to Budapest at 2,220 km is mostly exact. These distances are a little short: Rome to Helsinki—2,204 km; Kano, Nigeria to Liberia, Monrovia—2,215 km; Tokyo to Manila—2,204 km.

New Jerusalem spaceship size superimposed on the moon.

The dwarf planet, Pluto, is 1,472.65 miles (2,370 km) across—92 miles wider than the New Jerusalem or only 46 miles larger on each side.

Because Pluto is so far away, it is hard to imagine the comparison, so let us superimpose the New Jerusalem on our moon. The moon is 2,159 miles (3,474 km) in diameter or larger than the New Jerusalem by 779 miles or 389.5 miles (627 km) on each side. The figure above is what the New Jerusalem would look like if parked just above the surface of the moon. Big.

How high is 1,380 miles?

The International Space Station orbits at about 155 miles (250 km). If the cube ship landed on the earth (which it will never do), the top would interfere with the orbit of most satellites. Imagine the space station entering a hangar on the western side of the cube. As tractor beams bring it to a stop, the ship settles on an elevator and descends into a maintenance bay for routine repairs, resupply, and crew exchange. If the New Jerusalem had twelve floors, each 115 miles high, the space station would land somewhere *on the first floor.*

If this great ship moves into a low orbit, it will pull Earth's tides in different directions and create massive flooding on every coast. Fault lines will buckle under the great strain with earthquakes and volcanic eruptions along all tectonic seams. So where it parks will make a huge difference.

I am guessing that whoever is flying the ship will settle outside High Earth Orbit, outside the geocentrically orbiting weather satellites—22,000 miles away. Low Earth Orbit is 100 miles out (160 km), Medium Earth Orbit is 1,200 miles (2,000 km), Geosynchronous Orbit is 22,236 miles (35,700 km), with High Earth Orbit beyond. No matter where it parks, the ship will affect the earth, but if the ship comes closer, we will definitely lose satellites and the earth will experience a difference in the gravitational influence. Another thought: When the ship arrives, satellites will not matter anymore or what happens to the earth if too close, because the location in orbit will have another convenience in mind.

The Apostle John spends a lot of time explaining to us what the angel said and showed him, and the description of the city ship on the outside flows easily into what he describes on the inside.

How big is the inside?

To understand better how big the New Jerusalem is, let's compare it to Earth. Earth's total land mass (not including oceans) is about 57.3 million square miles with approximately 33 percent covered in desert and 24 percent of towering mountains, leaving only 24.6 million square miles of truly habitable land. Yes, a number of people do live in the other areas.

John tells us that the city—still describing the spaceship—has twelve foundations, which I suspect is his way of describing levels, because he is not talking about a building, or a temple, or steps leading up to something. Dividing 1,380 by twelve means each interior level is approximately 115 miles high. If one level were 1,904,400 square miles (1,380 x 1,380), then twelve levels (1,904,400 x 12) would give us 22,852,800 total square miles of floor space. At 22.8 million square miles, the New Jerusalem would be roughly equivalent to the earth's landmass today.

From any floor, you would not be able to see the ceiling; it would disappear into the blueness of the distance far, far above, similar to our sky now. At 29,029 feet (8,848 m), Mount Everest would fit easily on a single level. If you climbed to the top of the mountain—five and a half miles high, there would still be 109.5 miles (176 km) to the ceiling.

While Earth's atmosphere stretches to 300 miles high, most of it—80 percent—is within just ten miles, but easily breathable for only about three miles high. We drove up to the Pikes Peak summit outside Colorado Springs, Colorado—14,114 feet—a little more than two and a half miles. When we stepped out of the truck, we wobbled, unsteady on our legs. The altitude and lack of oxygen took some getting used to.

In the New Jerusalem, the oxygen content would be consistent from floor to ceiling, whatever the height, because it is an enclosed space with a controlled environment. In other words, the air would not get thinner as you climbed a mountain 29,000 feet high.

ALIENS, GOD, AND THE BIBLE

If all of this seems too big to imagine, it is because we think laterally—a floor with a 115-mile-high ceiling of great sky above—sounds like a lot of wasted space to me. Instead, we need to remember that life in the cube starship will probably be three-dimensional.

We know from scripture that the ship will have some kind of gravity—people walk on streets, sit in chairs, and water flows in rivers (Rev 22:1-6). But I believe the great space above each floor, however big, will be just as populated as the floor itself with objects, villages, people, animals, and, of course, passing clouds.

Even the walls and ceilings of each level might have a gravitational system, allowing people to live in those areas (on the walls and ceiling) while maximizing the livability of all "potential" floor, wall, and ceiling space. In other words, if it's "down" for you, then it is a floor.

The walls of each level are 115 miles high. Therefore, 1,380 x 115 would give us 158,700 square miles for one wall, or 634,800 square miles for all four walls—total wall space on a level. Add that to a floor of 1,904,400 square miles *and a ceiling of 1,904,400 square miles* and you have approximately 4,443,600 square miles of habitable land *per level*. Multiply that by twelve and you get 53,323,200 square miles of potentially habitable land for all levels in a three-dimensional cube—equivalent to a little more than two Earths.

I think there will be plenty of land to go around. If you are the type of person who needs a little space, then get onboard.

Why is the cube ship this big? Why are the levels so huge?

Is the cube so immense because the race of angels will live with us or on separate floors? We read that some angels have wings, so the three-dimensional space would be ideal for them. Yet, even we will fly: *"Who are these people who fly along like clouds, like doves to their nests?"* (Isaiah 60:8). So maybe we will be playing our harps (or acoustic guitars) among the clouds after all.

The rivers, streams, lakes, and ponds will have to be in closed systems, like my backyard pond. The little creek we made erupts from under a statue of Saint Francis holding a little bird and bowl of water, running downhill ten feet into the pond, where the pump sends it back to the top. Little waterfalls along the way make a wonderfully relaxing sound, while the pond supports a variety of plants and fish, not to mention the many wildlife visitors.

Likewise, the cube would have Earth weather. With ceilings 115 miles high, each level could have their own weather system—clouds, storms, winds, humidity—tailored to fit the inhabitant's particular needs or preferences. With the right equipment, someone could program weather changes into the system to allow for rain, occasional lightning, and winds of various speeds, in order to create a more natural climate and experience.

I like to think that thunderstorms will form high in the sky, especially with 115-mile-high levels. Where the storms move—closer to one side than another—will determine which surface enjoys the rain. Lightning and rain rid the atmosphere of dust and pollen pollutants, transform nitrogen into nitrogen oxides and nitric acid for a natural fertilizer, and cause some plants and trees to release their fragrant oils. I would enjoy a weekly thunderstorm, and I think the ecosystem would, too.

Revelation chapter 22 describes the River of the Water of Life, which flows from the throne of God right down the middle of the boulevard. The Tree of Life straddles the river, since we read that the tree is on both sides: *"On each side of the river stood the Tree of Life"* (Rev 22:2). The river is not flowing around it, as if the tree stood on an island.

Some have suggested that a straddling tree would make for an awkward-looking object, like a person straddling a small creek—not obviously efficient, and certainly not suitably dignified. However, when I imagine a great tree rising majestically above an equally worthy river, whose purpose is to bless all of humankind, I remember the tree on the planet Pandora from the movie *Avatar* (2009). Towering. Awe-inspiring. The Omaticaya tribe of the Na'vi people used the entire 500-foot-tall (150 m) tree. The people could climb in and on the tree, which served as the center of their culture. The Tree of Life would be such a tree. People on the New Jerusalem could fly up into the Tree of Life to pick the fruit and leaves alongside the birds.

Think big. Or maybe I should say, *think bigger.*

Imagine a tree at least one mile high—ten times higher than HomeTree on Pandora, comfortably straddling any river God placed beneath it. Is one mile too small for everyone who might want to use it? Then imagine a tree three miles high. With 115-mile-high ceilings, such a tree would feel right at home and comfortably tower over a river as wide as the Mississippi.

But why is the Tree of Life and the River of the Water of Life on the ship? We read that the tree's leaves are for the healing of the nations, and it provides a crop of fully ripened fruit each month.

> But blessed is the one who trusts in the Lord, whose confidence is in him. They will be like a tree planted by the water that sends out its roots by the stream. It does not fear when heat comes; its leaves are always green. It has no worries in a year of drought and never fails to bear fruit (Jeremiah 17:7-8).

Leaves are a sign of health. If Jesus is the main vine and we are the branches (John 15:5), then leaves are the way we breathe, thrive, and experience our relationship with God, other people, and enjoy abundant life. Spiritually, we absorb the Light of the Son, while transforming into his likeness and radiating our light (Matt 5:16).

Leaves for healing nations is not about actual or arbitrary lines on a map, but rather for healing relationships: hurting people, wherever they are found. We learn to hate, fear, and distrust. And we have all been hurt. These leaves are a balm whether eaten, applied as a salve, brewed in a tea, or burned and inhaled, bridging personal and national healing, mending, and restoration.

The prophet Ezekiel talks about something like this. Starting in chapter 43, he describes God's Glory returning to the Temple in Jerusalem and all that entails. He receives specific instructions for how to build the altar, how the priests, Levites, and people should act, and what to expect. In a vision, he described, *"water coming out from under the threshold of the temple . . ."* (Ezek 47:1). The river flowed from the temple, through the wilderness to the Dead Sea, where it turned salty water into fresh (Ezek 47:8). However, at the end, he says:

> Fruit trees of all kinds will grow on both banks of the river. Their leaves will not wither, nor will their fruit fail. Every month they will bear, because the water from the sanctuary flows to them. Their fruit will serve for food and their leaves for healing (Ezek 47:12).

This sounds similar to what happens on the New Jerusalem.

Ezekiel 43 and following describes how God wanted the Second Temple built, after the Jews returned from their seventy-year exile in Babylon. However, the river flowing to the Dead Sea and the fruit trees blessing the nations did not happen as described. The only possible time that this last part could take place—if we take the passage literally, is either during the thousand-year reign of Christ or after all of the great wars are over and the New Earth is created (Rev 21). This idea brings the New Jerusalem city in the heavens in line with something happening on the ground in Jerusalem, on Mount Zion.

Metaphorically, we can imagine Jesus being the Living Water, flowing out of the Temple to a "Dead Sea" of people in great need, living in darkness, who will see this Great Light and experience refreshment and healing by believing in him. Isaiah wrote:

For I will pour water on the thirsty land, and streams on the dry ground; I will pour out my Spirit on our offspring and blessings on your descendants" (Isaiah 44:3).

Instead of plucking fruit off a literal tree, we experience the outpouring of the Spirit, partake of and produce the Fruit of the Spirit, while living in the Kingdom of God—now (Galatians 5:22-23).

John tells us that the Tree of Life and the River of the Water of Life will be on the New Jerusalem. Will they be a benefit to the citizens living there? Why do immortal people need this river and tree? If John saw and described these things, then they must be important. Will there be passengers on the ship who are mortal, or children born on the New Jerusalem who are mortal? Will angels or people dispense the fruit and leaves of this tree and the water from the river to those in need on other planets, wherever the ship travels in the universe?

Sometimes it is not possible to discern whether something is real as described in the Bible, or a metaphor, or both. For some things, we can only wait and see. The presence of the tree and river raise more questions than answers at this time; some answers we will not know until we are there.

Let me take a minute to talk about another tree in relation to this great ship. In Genesis 2, we read that God created a Garden in a place called Eden. In the middle were two trees: the Tree of Life and the Tree of the Knowledge of Good and Evil. When God placed Adam in the Garden of Eden (before Eve was created), he told Adam he could eat of any trees in the Garden but to *not touch or eat* of the Tree of the Knowledge of Good and Evil (Gen 2:15-17). Now we read that the Tree of Life is on the New Jerusalem, but there is no mention of the Tree of Knowledge, that other tree in the Garden. What does this mean?

God designed the great ship for us, presented as a type of benefit for humans who lived on Earth, who once bore the curse of Adam and Eve's disobedience (original sin).

Therefore, just as sin entered the world through one man (Adam), *and death through sin, and in this way death came to all people, because all sinned* (Romans 5:12).

Humans who live on the ship have already learned the difference between good and evil: They were born, lived, and died under the curse of Adam, but were able to gain admission by choosing the Good—Jesus (Romans 5:15). I know this is a little simplistic, but overall a true statement. So that other tree in the Garden, the Tree of the Knowledge of Good and Evil, served its purpose in the Garden long ago and is not needed on the ship.

We read that humans, while living on Earth, are *a little lower than the angels* (Heb 2:7-9), as exemplified by the life of Jesus. However, in 1 Cor 6:3, Paul tells us we will judge the angels. I wonder if our knowledge and experience of good and evil means we will be a slightly greater race—relatively speaking, post resurrection. Does it mean that our difference, having lived under the curse, is somehow valuable to God—his goals and purposes—in the future?

COMPOSITION

It shone with the glory of God, and its brilliance was like that of a very precious jewel, like jasper, clear as crystal (Rev 21:11).

God could make the ship out of anything he wanted, and he chose something that *appeared like jasper.* It must be important. I wonder if there are peculiar properties in relation to this mineral or gem that would make it better suited for the skin of a great ship instead of some type of metal: The space industry often uses titanium, aluminum, stainless steel, and nickel.

Jasper comes in many colors: dark pink to red being most common. "Like jasper" is not jasper, while "clear as crystal" suggests another gem—diamond.

I am guessing that John did not know about pink diamonds, so he described what he saw based on what he knew—*the color of jasper but clear.* If the walls were actually reddish or pink diamond, extremely rare and hard, that would make a formidable outer skin for this starship and fit John's description perfectly.

The strongest material in the world—at this time—just happens to be diamond nanothreads, which are stronger and stiffer than any other known substance.[1] Imagine a wall two hundred feet thick composed of pink diamond nanothread-like material. This wall would be able to withstand the heat and radiation of outer space and the pressures exerted on it from the interior artificial gravity systems and exterior force fields. In fact, with this nanotech substance, the outer walls and interior levels or floors would be a seamless structure.

When traveling in deep space, geomagnetic storms, solar energetic particles, and galactic cosmic radiation deal a continuous dose of radiation to people riding on a spaceship and can cause sickness and eventually death. I find it interesting that diamond nanothread walls filled with hydrogen, boron, and nitrogen gases would better protect living things inside from these cosmic rays than a typical metal wall.[2]

Because of the nature of nanothreads, the diamond wall might also have healing properties, capable of self-sealing after a meteor impact. The "wound" would recover from the damage, because technicians could realign the nanothreads to repair or replace damaged sections. The nanothreads might even have that capability built in—self-healing.[3] The ship's skin would always look new: something I think God would prefer.

The Bible describes twelve primary gates, but the manipulation of the nanothreads would enable hatches and ports in the skin to open and close so people and ships could enter and exit at different points all along the walls, ceilings, and floors. Typical ship construction would include passageways, pipes, tubes, conduits, vents, ducting, hatches, and gates. The nanothreads could easily create these in the floors and walls. In other words, parts of the walls, floors, and ceilings would become hollow piping as determined by ship needs.

A diamond skin would also make the ship lighter than any other metallic materials—more than one hundred times the strength of steel at a fraction of the weight. So although the great spaceship is 1,380 miles square, the angel tells John the outer wall needs to be only 144 cubits or 208 feet thick (63.4 meters), probably because of the diamond structure, composition, and construction. Simply amazing.

STAR SHIP

CHAPTER TWO

INTERIOR

FOUNDATIONS

The wall of the city had twelve foundations . . . (Rev 21:14).

The Greek word used for *"foundations"* is themelios, which literally means "a thing laid down, associated with foundation, base, groundwork, infrastructure."

For example, Paul tells Timothy:

> *. . . if I am delayed, you will know how people ought to conduct themselves in God's household, which is the church of the living God, the pillar and foundation of the truth* (1 Timothy 3:15, also 2 Timothy 2:19).

Foundational. Basic. Supporting. The foundations are levels in the city, New Jerusalem, because they are supporting infrastructure. We might think of them better as floors, while sailors on this great ship will call them decks. Someone suggested that if John wanted to use the word *floors,* he could have. The problem is the size. If it were a building, floors would be appropriate. However, we are talking about an object as large as a small planet. Each level could support jungles, forests, seas, prairie, and desert landscapes, and even mountain ranges.

We do not know how thick each level is. I would not assume they are only two hundred feet thick like the outer walls, but that would be a place to start, providing an overall continuity and style. But God could strategically place support pillars between the floors: perhaps a few under a mountain range on the level above. These massive columns could be multi-use structures. Column interior ducting and elevators would transport water, power, and supplies. How would you like to have an apartment in a column with a balcony at the one-mile level, overlooking a vast green belt of forests, meadows, and ponds?

Here is another clue that the outer hull of the ship is diamond. John does not mention this invaluable gem in the foundations—rare and highly prized during the time of the Roman empire.

> *The first foundation was JASPER* (shades of pink to red), *the second SAPPHIRE* (many colors, but light to dark blue most common), *the third CHALCEDONY* (milky white or blue to light gray), *the fourth EMERALD* (a type of beryl–light green), *the fifth SARDONYX* (variety of chalcedony–red brown, often with white stripes), *the sixth CARNELIAN* (dark orange to red), *the seventh CHRYSOLITE* (also known as peridot–yellow green to green), *the eighth BERYL* (also known as Aquamarine–blue green), *the ninth TOPAZ* (comes in a variety of colors, but topaz from the Middle East is light blue and sparkles like water), *the tenth CHRYSOPRASE* (grass green), *the eleventh JACINTH* (a.k.a. hyacinth–blue violet), *and the twelfth AMETHYST* (blue or mauve to purple) (Rev 21:19-20).

Diamond nanothreads, sapphire nanothreads—perhaps they are all the same to God. In this passage, John does not say the first foundation is *like jasper*, this time he says it is jasper. In the first century, people identified gems and stones by color, so a red gem could be garnet, jasper, or ruby, depending on who was describing the piece.

However, John is quite specific, describing stones he seems to be familiar with, or identified with the angel's coaching. Is John's description of these gems the same as what we know today? I am thinking of the difference in the Roman mile and English statute mile. We can only guess at the true colors John viewed, and most of the gems above come in a wide variety.

While in Thunder Bay, Ontario, Canada, I was able to dig for amethyst at a mine. In just the one rock, there were colors ranging from clear to black, with every shade of blue and purple in between. We cannot know the exact colors John saw, although we recognize the most popular versions. What I do know is that these luminous foundations will be amazing and beautiful: a rainbow of colors reflecting light and dazzling our eyes.

Amethyst in its raw form. Note the variations from the edges toward the center—light to dark.

Amethyst - Blue to Purple

Jacinth - Blue Violet

Chrysophrase - Lt Green

Topaz - Lt Blue

Beryl - Aquamarine

Chrysolite - Yellow Green to Green

Carnelian - Lt Orange to Red

Sardonyx - Red Brown

Emerald - Green

Chalcedony - Lt Blue

Sapphire - Blue

Jasper - Pink to Red

This cube represents the New Jerusalem, and the lines are the foundation levels, evenly spaced at approximately 115 mile intervals. (Note the appropriate colors in the descriptions.)

What do you notice first about the lines in this primitive image I made of the New Jerusalem? The floor or base of the cube is pinkish to red Jasper, which I believe signifies the shed blood of the Lamb. All levels rise above this literal and symbolic foundation.

Right in the middle, a line stands out—the sixth level, orange to red—carnelian. Carnelian comes from the Latin *carnis* for "flesh." *"The Word (Jesus) became flesh and lived for a while among us"* (John 1:14). The number six is the number of humans, with biblical references. For example, God created Adam on the sixth day. Whatever else is going on, I suspect that this level represents humankind as resurrected saints. Perhaps this level is the primary living space for the people of Earth.

The top level is bluish purple amethyst, the color of royalty. Could it be that this is the actual location of God's throne with the streets of gold and the River of Life and Tree of Life? All levels rest under this one, literally and symbolically.

I am guessing that the amethyst foundation will be for the Apostle John (Rev 21:19—an Apostle represents each level), because the jasper level will be reserved for the Apostle Peter, who had a foundational name and calling.

> And I tell you, you are Peter, and on this rock (foundation) I will build my church, and the gates of hell shall not prevail against it (Matthew 16:18, English Standard Version, ESV).

The carnelian level fits exactly in between the blood of the Sacrificial Lamb and the Risen Lamb—between the red and purple, while taking on reddish tones itself. A symbol of both humble subjection to our LORD, covered in the blood of the Lamb, and our place—centered in the scheme of things—perhaps central to God's plans and purposes.

Wax does not stick to carnelian, so leaders used it in signet rings for sealing letters and as a symbol of a ruler's authority and unchangeable decrees. Skilled artists would carve the leader's likeness or symbol into the gem then mount it in a ring.

In the book of Daniel, King Darius and his nobles sealed the lion's den with their signet rings (Daniel 6:17). Queen Jezebel sealed and sent letters in King Ahab's name to the elders and leaders of Jezreel, so Naboth's vineyard could be stolen from him and turned into a royal vegetable garden (1 Kings 21:1-14).

Then we come to Zerubbabel, grandson of King Jehoiachin. In the book of Jeremiah, God said, " . . . *if you, Jehoiachin—were a signet ring on my right hand, I would still pull you off"* (Jeremiah 22:24-27). God is disappointed in King Jehoiachin, but later sees something special in his grandson.

In the writings of the prophet Haggai, God said:

> *"Tell Zerubbabel governor of Judah that I will shake the heavens and the earth—On that day," declares the LORD Almighty, "I will take you, my servant Zerubbabel son of Shealtiel," declares the LORD, "and I will make you like my signet ring, for I have chosen you," declares the LORD Almighty* (Haggai 2:21-23).

My Servant is a reference to the Messiah (Isaiah 42:1-13, 52:13; Matthew 12:18). We read in Zechariah, a prophet from the same time period as Haggai, that Zerubbabel, the governor, and Joshua, the high priest, " . . . *are men symbolic of things to come: I am going to bring my servant, the branch* (Jesus Christ—see also Isaiah 11:1; Jeremiah 23:5-6), " . . . *and I will remove the sin of this land in a single day"* (reference to the Crucifixion—Zechariah 3:8-9).

I think the Apostle Paul must have been thinking of the signet ring mentioned by the prophet Zechariah, when he wrote this:

Now it is God who makes both us and you stand firm in Christ. He anointed us, set his seal of ownership on us, and put his Spirit in our hearts as a deposit, guaranteeing what is to come (2 Cor 1:21-22).

Seal and Ownership. I can imagine a special and unique ring on God's finger in the likeness of the Lamb, dipped in his sacrificial blood and pressed upon our hearts. Therefore, it is most appropriate that the carnelian foundation represents us.

GOLD

The wall was made of jasper, and the city of pure gold, as pure as glass (Rev 21:18).
The street of the city was of pure gold, like transparent glass (Rev 21:21).

In John's description, gold seems to be everywhere, especially in the streets, pure and transparent as glass. While the walls and foundations were constructed of different gems, pure transparent gold covers the floors and perhaps other things.

When John says the gold is pure, he means 24-karat with no alloys mixed in such as copper, silver, or platinum. Even raw gold is not often that pure. Jewelry makers use alloys to make the gold harder and more durable for wear. For example, 18-karat gold is 25 percent copper. The angel must have told John this gold was 100 percent pure.

Transparent gold?

Am I the only one who finds it incredible that John is describing transparent gold in the first century? I cannot say John was the first science *fiction* writer, because the Book of Revelation is not fiction. Would that genre be science prophecy?

Making transparent gold is an involved process first developed around 1922. To obtain a film 1/798,000 of an inch thick—10,500 times thinner than a sheet of paper, gold is placed on a thin copper plate in an electric bath, which causes it to spread out evenly. To separate the gold, the copper plate is immersed in nitric acid, which dissolves the copper and leaves the thin sheet of gold floating on the surface. I am thinking God does not have to go through all of this to make transparent gold.

We have looked at diamond nanotechnology for the walls and foundations, so would you be surprised to learn that scientists have developed gold nanomesh—*transparent and stretchable*. If there is a lot of foot traffic around the throne of God, I think a surface that gives a little might make a better floor covering in the New Jerusalem.

BENEFITS OF TRANSPARENT GOLD
First, gold does not tarnish. Second, gold is heavy—in a starship where mass, inertia, and gravity are constant concerns, thinner gold is better. Third, gold is also a great reflector of

light, heat, and radiation, which is why the space industry uses transparent gold for the space helmet visor. Fourth, with hints of red, gold is dazzling and beautiful.

For the New Jerusalem, gold has practical applications and theological significance, representing faith, the unchangeableness of God, and the purity of grace, while hints of red point to the redeeming work of the Lamb on the cross.

Gold is the "asphalt" of choice in heaven, because it does not tarnish or require maintenance like other metals and materials. If in a nanomesh type of configuration, the floor may even have healing properties like the outer skin and foundations of the ship. This is important because a single ounce of gold can be made so thin it covers 300 square meters.

Imagine the bluish-purple amethyst floor of the Royal Throne level, a dazzling blue with shades of purple reflected throughout. Standing on that floor would be like walking on a great sea of water, so you could look down into the sparkling depths. Now apply a microscopically thin covering of gold and witness the subtle color shift to a pale green. Breathtaking. Preeminent. *"Also before the throne there was what looked like a sea of glass, clear as crystal"* (Rev 4:6). There you go.

The periodic chart symbol for gold is AU, from the Latin name for gold, *aurum*, which means "Glow of Sunrise." Is that an appropriate name for the floor covering before the Throne of God? Jesus said he was the Bright and Morning Star (Rev 22:16), which would mean he is also the First Glow of Sunrise. Moreover, we are supposed to walk on it: another reason why we have to take off our shoes, if we wear them at all. God told Moses:

Take off your sandals, for the place where you are standing is holy ground (Exodus 3:5; Joshua 5:15).

The sea of glass before the Throne of God will certainly be holy ground.

BRIGHT AND MORNING STAR

Jupiter, Venus, and Mars are our bright morning "stars" when their orbits place them on the horizon at the right time. However, our sun is the brightest true star rising in the east, which brings warmth, nourishment, and blessing while driving the darkness away—Peter understood this.

We also have the message of the prophets, which has been confirmed beyond doubt. And you will do well to pay attention to this message, as to a Lamp shining in a dark place, until the Day Dawns and the Morning Star rises in your hearts (2 Peter 1:19, Berean Study Bible).

Do not be confused. With this talk of foundations and levels, John is *not* describing a city within the cube, but the cube itself. Revelation 21:22 tells us that there is no need for a great building in the cube *". . . because the LORD God Almighty and the Lamb are its temple."*

Then what is it people see, who experience near-death experiences, who go to heaven for a short time and describe a real city with pearly gates?

I believe many of these people visited the spiritual place we call heaven and saw a city with a wall and gates of pearl. But they were not describing a spaceship. Heaven is a separate place and dimension where God dwells. Apparently, God has modeled and configured the New Jerusalem after the system and structure in heaven, which does not surprise me, since in the future, God moves from his heavenly abode to the starship.

The Bible has described this idea before—something modeled after heaven. Speaking of the tabernacle Moses built in the wilderness (Exodus 35), the author of Hebrews wrote:

> *They* (the priests and Levites) *serve at a sanctuary that is a copy and shadow of what is in heaven* (the tabernacle design and contents). *This is why Moses was warned when he was about to build the tabernacle: "See to it that you make everything according to the pattern shown you on the mountain"* (Hebrews 8:5, referring to Exodus 25:40).

Copy and shadows. Types and shadows.

Like the tabernacle, the New Jerusalem design is based on similar, or the same objects and ideas, found in the spiritual place we know as heaven.

Have you heard of solar tube lighting? A lens on the roof captures sunlight from different directions and sends it down a metal tube of highly-reflective material. The natural light brightens dark rooms in the house, reducing the need for electricity without adding heat. Efficient. Easy. In like manner, I can imagine the Light of God emanating from the top level—the Throne Room. This Light moves through the diamond nanothread walls into the gem foundations, so that Light pours into every corner of every level, while also causing the outside of the New Jerusalem to glow brightly.

> *The city* (New Jerusalem) *does not need the sun or the moon to shine on it, for the glory of God gives it light, and the Lamb is its Lamp. The nations will walk by its light* . . . (Rev 21:23-24).

As this great crystal ship moves into orbit, it will glow but not by reflecting sunlight and moonlight. The New Jerusalem will be a light source, illuminating the earth during the night, because the walls are relatively thin and clear as crystal, allowing God's Light to flow outward. The city's brilliance will rival our sun during the day without generating additional heat to the planet's surface. A truly Bright and Morning star, whose Light the nations will literally walk in.

Looking up to see the New Jerusalem reminds me of Moses and the children of Israel during their forty-year march through the wilderness. They could look up at the cloud.

> *By day the LORD went ahead of them in a pillar of cloud to guide them on their way and by night in a pillar of fire to give them light, so that they could travel by day or night. Neither the pillar of cloud by day nor the pillar of fire by night left its place in front of the people* (Exodus 13:21-22).

We get up early, before sunrise, and go outside. The morning stars shine brightly in the starry black expanse. In the east, we see a colorful flash. Light shoots through the high wispy clouds so that rainbow rays shoot across our sky. The great ship rises slowly above the horizon, and we stop what we are doing to watch, intently, in awe. Smiling. The sky begins to brighten, throwing yellow, orange, and red glows on the clouds all around us—spreading, reaching. But wait! The New Jerusalem glow is causing this wonderful display, because the sun will not rise for another hour!

The sun will no more be your light by day, nor will the brightness of the moon shine on you, for the LORD will be your everlasting Light, and your God will be your glory (Isaiah 60:19).

PEARLS

John describes twelve gates—three on each side of the cube—made of a single great pearl with at least one angel guard posted nearby. For centuries, many cultures have used pearls to treat infertility and issues related to the eye, heart, liver, digestive tract, skin, and muscle. Some believe wearing pearls has a calming effect and balances our biometrics and good will. Pearls bring lots of symbolism.

Why pearl gates? Probably because the city walls in heaven have gates of pearl. Of all the elements described that make up the New Jerusalem, the pearl gate comes from a living creature in layers of beauty, purity, and iridescence. Unlike rock and mineral gems, God fabricates the organic pearl, which does not need to be carved or polished to improve the appearance. The pearl gates would be unique in all respects and in the entire universe. Only God can create them.

Did you ever wonder what God might consider the most beautiful inanimate object he ever created? Certainly, the pink diamond would top the list, but it has to be cut and polished to reveal the hidden beauty. Instead, the perfectly round pearl might be his favorite based on what we discover in the Bible.

When he calls to us, *"Come and share your master's happiness!"* (Matt 25:21), we must pass through an iridescent gem, a pearl—the city gate in heaven or, in the future, the port into the New Jerusalem—a pearl of unimaginable great price, rarity, and beauty (Matt 13:45-46). A symbol of our transformation derived from a living thing, yet with allusions to baptism, resurrection, and grace.

From a grain of sand, the oyster creates a pearl by covering the irritant in layers of itself: a substance called nacre (pronounced *nāker*). Does God create a pearl by covering the irritant called sin with layers of himself—grace, blood, and love?—an appropriate entryway into his presence. One we can only enter by accepting the transforming action of his grace, blood, and love in our lives (Romans 12:1-2). Pearl of great price, indeed.

GATES

Let me explain something before we go on. I struggled with this gate configuration for a long time, until I discovered an idea sitting right in front of me. Yes, the gate is made of pearl, *but there are no doors.* Speaking of the spaceship, we read, *"On no day will its gates ever be shut, for there will be no night there"* (Rev 21:25).

Arc de Triomphe.
Permission: aviewoncities.com.

Imagine something like the Arc de Triomphe in Paris, created as a single tremendous pearl, mounted on the side of the New Jerusalem spaceship's outer wall-hull—a gate portal without gate doors. The whole gate would be 208 feet deep from outside to inside, and force fields would control the openings—outside and inside. That is probably why an angel is dedicated to each gate: a Pearl Gate Engineer.

A force field?

If God can create artificial gravity on the inside, don't you think he could create localized force fields on the outside? People would arrive in a ship and simply pass through the gate entrance—with the angel's permission, of course (Rev 21:27), then travel down the passageway to the inside.

The gates would be immense. If a wall 1,380 miles high and wide staggers your imagination, would you be perplexed if I suggested that each pearl gate opening was *only* twelve miles high and twelve miles wide? From a distance, these gates would still appear as mere dots on the side of the ship.

Twelve miles? You will notice in the Bible that the number twelve (and variables 3, 72, 144) has special meaning to God: twelve gates, twelve foundations, twelve tribes of Israel, twelve apostles, the walls at 144 cubits (12x12), the city size 12,000 furlongs, and more, appearing 187 times—twenty-two "twelves" just in the book of Revelation.

There are twelve levels and twelve gates.

Where would the gate locations be? Originally, I thought it would be simple—one through three on the north side, four through six on the west, etc. But while studying nacre, I saw an image of the nautilus and the idea of a spiral gate formation came to mind. I can imagine Gate 1 on the north side, at the top. Then move right to the next side and down one level for Gate 2, then right and down a level for Gate 3, and so on, spiraling around the cube with Gate 12 on the bottom. So gates one, five, and nine would be on the north-facing side.

Every version I made of the pearl gate looked like a button, because I started with a round pearl, which is the most difficult to create in nature—and the most valuable. Pearls come in every possible shape and color. I thought the pearl gate would be uniform and simple—round. We'll see.

The gates are named after the tribes of Israel. I wonder if the Judah Gate will give us entrance to the Royal Throne level at the top (Rev 21:12), since Jesus is called the Lion of Judah and is from that tribe: *"Behold, the Lion of the tribe of Judah, the Root of David, has triumphed"* (Rev 5:5). However laid out, your travels or final destination inside the New Jerusalem will probably determine which gate you use.

So I believe all of this is real, even if the size, nature, and purpose of these objects can scarcely be imagined, or understood. John, a fisherman turned disciple of the first century, did his best to describe his vision for us and honestly wrote down everything he saw no matter how fantastic.

But why is the spaceship so big? That would depend on its purpose, wouldn't it?

SCOPE

=== CHAPTER THREE ===

AND

PURPOSE

Many authors have written books and movies about space travel. The dangers and wonders generate series like *Star Wars* and *Star Trek*. We cannot get enough; well, some of us can't. The scale of the New Jerusalem is incredible and few stories have anything like it.

The nature of science fiction is based on our imagination reaching into realms we are often unfamiliar with. If the story has talking animals, we call it fantasy. But if the engines come on and move the ship into the void of space, the technology of the fictional work determines the genre and we call it science fiction. Something like that is happening in the Book of Revelation.

The angel showed John the future, then John wrote down what he saw, revealing his vision—a revelation. Not from his imagination, but as events unfolded, often with explanations from his angel guide. The events he describes are not always in order, either as envisioned, or later in the way he wrote the scenes. Whatever is happening in the telling of this End Times apocalyptic story, when he is all done, a great starship is sitting in orbit above Earth. Therefore, I feel compelled to speculate on its potential purposes.

GENERATIONAL STARSHIP

Is the New Jerusalem a multi-generational starship for traveling great distances across the Milky Way, and perhaps to other galaxies? If the ship cannot travel faster than the speed of light due to relativistic constraints (reference Einstein's speed of light travel limitations), generations would come and go over thousands of years on a galactic journey to other stars and habitable planets. Generations of people would learn to call the great ship home.

IMMUNOLOGY

One reason for the many levels could be to keep our immune systems intact, so we could survive an alien planet's microbial defense systems. Do you remember the movie *War of the Worlds*, and how Earth's bacteria killed off the Martian invaders? If we are seeding other planets, the population would need to remain healthy, vigorous, and growing. The Tree of Life would keep people healthy (and immortal), but probably not if they disembarked to colonize other planets.

CONTINUITY

One group could continue to pilot the ship, while others became colonists. Perhaps each new generation would take control of the ship, while the previous group gave up that chore to colonize the planet. A few people would remain as the core base of knowledge and skill—perhaps the ship's captain and select volunteer crew.

However, if the passengers are immortal, that raises a completely new set of questions. I assume the immortal passengers would have children. Jesus does say that in heaven people do not marry *like on earth* (Matt 22:30); but I do not think that applies to a spaceship, especially if colonization is the goal. So would people have kids? Would we reunite with our earthly spouse, or would another system prevail as described by Jesus? I mean, what if you were in an abusive relationship on Earth? Would the children borne of resurrected parents automatically have the same characteristics and abilities?—the ability to appear and disappear, fly, immortality? Would parents need to discipline children? Would their teenagers be like teenagers on Earth?

LOGISTICS

Would God provide for all necessary logistical and material concerns? For a season, I was the logistics officer in an army battalion. I loved that job, especially the complex challenges associated with moving the battalion—people and equipment—from the United States to Germany for a REFORGER (Return of Forces to Europe) exercise. Transportation, fuel, lodging, waste, water, and food at each stage of the movement tested my multi-tasking mind and staff.

However, as I studied the New Jerusalem, I realized that many of my concerns for regular human activities might not apply here. What would God provide? God has the habit of providing the basic substance—seeds, soil, air, water—while we do the work of planting, nurturing, and harvesting. Would sections of the New Jerusalem be set aside for agriculture and farming, and water capture, transport, treatment, and recycling?

WINE WITH CHEESE AND CRACKERS

On this mountain the Lord Almighty will prepare a feast of rich food for all peoples, a banquet of aged wine—the best of meats and the finest of wines (Isaiah 25:6).

I think God appreciates a fine aged wine and well-cooked rib-eye steak. But while the feasting referenced here might take place on Mount Zion, I wonder if we will have similar food choices on the New Jerusalem. Would we keep vineyards? Vineyards would require the infrastructure for processing the grapes into wine, and then bottling and transportation.

And what about meat? It seems that Adam and Eve were vegetarians, because we read that after the Fall, God provided them with skins for clothing, and the animal sacrifice system started outside the Garden. So would the spaceship passengers harken to the earlier age of Garden innocence and be vegetarians? If vegetarians, would we still keep herds to produce milk products? Or chickens for eggs? I find it hard to imagine a lemon meringue pie without the meringue. Then we have the poor Scots. What will they do if they can't get haggis; a pudding made of sheep's heart, liver, and lungs? Poor lads.

Nevertheless, despite our favorite foods and drinks on this planet, we will be satisfied and pleased with whatever God provides on the spaceship.

WASTE

We read that Jesus provides a feast in heaven.

Then he said to me, "Write, Blessed are those who are invited to the marriage supper of the Lamb" (Rev 18:9).

Do people in resurrected bodies defecate? Perhaps heavenly food is spiritual. Taste, smell, and texture are present, the sensation of chewing and swallowing, but nothing actually rests in the stomach. You drink an aged wine, but drunkenness is not possible. You eat all night, but are not full.

But I do not think this will be the case on the New Jerusalem. This ship is real, in the physical universe, and it will have a real infrastructure. We will be there with real bodies that require food, sleep, and elimination options—defecation. Would we use a type of toilet and toilet paper? Some ship passengers—resurrected people—will not have had the experience of a modern toilet or toilet paper. Or even coffee, for that matter—ouch.

I would imagine that a standardized ship-wide system of waste management would be in effect. Perhaps angel guides will show us how to live on the ship, if these systems are in place when we arrive. I mean, the ship is futuristic and the waste system will probably be just as sophisticated with recycling options we can't imagine.

TRANSPORTATION AND FARMING

Have you ever had flying dreams? I have. Many. In my dreams, I fly in a seated position with my feet facing forward. Probably looks odd, but landing is certainly more natural. I can imagine everyone flying, but we would need other transportation options: a fleet of ground vehicles for farming, smaller anti-gravity shuttles, and ships for traveling from Earth to the Cube. Imagine a fleet of smaller crystalline cube-shaped craft for interior and exterior travel.

I cannot imagine vehicles using fossil fuels—gasoline, diesel, and oil. Fossil fuel oil and gas is harvested from the earth, then processed and refined into different products. Some other method of propulsion must be at work with vehicles in the ship. If the technology is in place for anti-gravity lifting and hovering, it could be used for movement also. So even if the farmer's field was plowed with something like a beam of light, the seeds need to be planted, the crop harvested, then sent somewhere for processing.

But here I am—anxious about commercial farming. I do not think Adam and Eve worried about commercial farming in the Garden. So perhaps God will scatter the necessary seeds for food and we will graze at our leisure. We'll gather at a patch of corn growing on the east wall of level seven. Then as the mood strikes us, we'll wander over to where the grapes grow wild near the corn, along with miles of soybeans and trees of tea. Grazing sounds idyllic, if we are concerned about food at all. But if you want a cup of hot chocolate, an involved process unfolds in front of you. Perhaps we just need to imagine what we want, and it appears—a spiritual food synthesizer. "Eight ounce coffee, Ethiopian Sumatran blend, 170 degrees." Sounds like a Starbucks order on the Starship *Enterprise*.

MAINTENANCE

Things break. Equipment wears down. Normal for machinery. Over a million years of continuous use, even ceramic parts and a self-healing ship's skin might need servicing. What maintenance tasks and responsibilities would the residents have in relation to this journey? How would tasks and assignments be set? Would we all rotate through various jobs and responsibilities? How would a growing population challenge food production, waste disposal, or systems for air, water, and recycling? In time, we could probably have a *Dirtiest Jobs* episode on the ship.

Repairs—inside and outside—create their own challenges. Do angels need special equipment to work in the vacuum of space? Would we need special equipment to work outside in our new immortal bodies? I mean, do the laws of physics apply to humans in their immortal, resurrection form? If we can fly, and appear and disappear like Jesus, perhaps the laws of physics do not apply—or not entirely. I wonder if we will have to physically turn a wrench to tighten a bolt or just "will it" to happen. "Be tight." If something needs tightening, would I use my mind to do it or bring along a tool bag with a Craftsman crescent wrench inside?

COMPOSITION

A ship this large could have multiple ecosystems with some levels set aside just for food production, another for grasslands, another for seas, and the creatures that thrive in each. If gravity is manipulated and controlled, one whole level could be a giant fish tank—aquarium. With artificial gravity, seas and ponds could be on the floor of a level—the traditional location, but also along the walls. I can imagine great bubbles wobbling around in the sky, merging, breaking apart, floating endlessly, each with populations of fish and sea creatures. That would take farm fishing—aqua fishing or pisciculture—to a completely new level.

Wouldn't it be fun to swim in a great bubble with fish? I skin dive. Swimming with dolphins in a bubble, shooting out into the sky, flying around the frothy blob of water, or jumping from bubble to bubble, then diving back in would be an endless joy.

DELIBERATION
(SOMETHING TO CONSIDER OR REFLECTION)

The problem with all of these questions is that God could just make things and make things happen: He is God after all. But that idea flies in the face of our obvious presence, and our intrinsic need to be intimately involved. And we will be involved.

BATTLE CRUISER

Another purpose might be military-related.

"That's no moon, it's a space station!" Obi-Wan said in *Star Wars Episode 4: A New Hope.*

The first Death Star space station was about 100 miles (160 km) across. The second Death Star was supposed to be 560 miles (900 km) in diameter—insignificant beside the New Jerusalem. Now you know Lando Calrissian flew the *Millennium Falcon* 280 miles through the superstructure to reach the core and then had to escape in time as the battle station exploded behind him. He barely made it.

For his immense arrogance, opposition to God, and evil actions, Satan was cast out of heaven to the earth (Isaiah 14:12; Rev 12:7-9). Heaven and the spiritual plane became a battleground with Earth at the epicenter. In that light, the Cube could be a battle cruiser or a troop carrier in the ongoing fight.

What ongoing fight?

The universe is a huge place. Is this the only planet where Satan has declared war on God and his creation? Could other planets be in conflict?

So many angels fell:

His tail swept a third of the stars out of the sky and flung them to earth (Rev 12:4, 9).

I was in the Army, so I wondered if these angels were willing accomplices in Satan's rebellion or were some of them swept along by events they had no control over, akin to soldiers following the orders of their superiors? If his tail "swept and flung" them, would that mean that some were unwilling soldiers of the rebellion—collateral damage?

Does the word "star" work as a metaphor here or do these angels actually represent stars, and by extension, habitable solar systems? I have wondered if each angel was a prince of their own star system and planets the way Satan is described as the prince of this planet.

In John 14:30 Jesus said, "*I will not say much more to you, for the prince of this world is coming…*" The prince of *this* world. Peculiar phrasing. It almost sounds like he could have said there is a prince of *this* world, and there is a prince of *that* world, and another, and another.

Are all of these Star Princes on Earth now? Alternatively, are some scattered among the stars and planets of our immense universe with populations of people, and perhaps the race of angels, requiring intervention and assistance from those already liberated—one planet at a time, one solar system at a time? Could this craft be a battle ship for warriors combating the fallen angels in other systems and even other dimensions?

If the enemy also has battle stations, I would want mine to be overwhelmingly large and intimidating; the conspicuous presence of which would bring unconditional surrender as it entered the star system. The New Jerusalem is certainly that.

I am not suggesting that Jesus (through the incarnation) would need to live and die on multiple planets, as he did here. Satan seems to be the main antagonist in this story and needed to be dealt with directly.

CONTRADICTIONS

But I cannot imagine the New Jerusalem bristling with weapons. New Jerusalem means *New City of Peace*. While Jesus is referred to as the Prince of Peace (Isa 9:6), he is the one who leads the *armies* of heaven to Earth (Rev 19:14). Armies—plural. Is this a contradiction? Because he is omniscient, God knows when to use military force and when not. At times, he even deplores the use of weapons.

"Some trust in chariots and some in horses, but we trust in the Name of the LORD our God" (Psalm 20:7), and this spoken by the premier warrior of his time, David. We might use things like chariots and we might ride creatures like horses, but how and when we go to battle is based on our faith and trust in God. The idea is that our true strength is not in these or any other war machines, but in God. And he has a plan and purpose for us and the New Jerusalem.

David understood something about the LORD and fighting and trusting, giving God all the credit. Although a short, audacious teenager, he killed a lion and bear who had stolen his sheep. Killing predators is one thing; going after hungry beasts with the prize in their mouths is quite another.

Although a strong young man, he also understood—at an intimate level—that it was God who gave him those victories.

> Then David said to the Philistine, (Goliath) *"You come to me with a sword, a spear, and a javelin, but I come to you in the Name of the LORD of Hosts, the God of the Armies of Israel, whom you have taunted"* (1 Samuel 17:45).

God spoke of this himself:

> Woe to those who go down to Egypt for help and rely on horses, and trust in chariots because they are many and in horsemen because they are very strong, but they do not look to the Holy One of Israel, nor seek the LORD! (Isaiah 31:1).

Why is this true? Because whether now or in the future, our ultimate success comes when we trust in God, especially against fearful odds. And yet, we boast in our pride, and brag about our influence, power, and smarts. We train for war. We are warriors. Children of fighters. We imagine that we can defeat any enemy—problem, dispute, competitor, obstacle, illness, pain—with our own strength. We shout, "I am the captain of my fate! Look at my wonderful success! What has God got to do with anything?" I have been guilty of this at times. More often than I would like to admit.

> I will punish the king of Assyria for the willful pride of his heart and the haughty look in his eyes. For he says, "By the strength of my hand I have done this, and by my wisdom, because I have understanding" (Isaiah 10:12–13).

Where were all of the mighty warriors of Israel when Goliath stepped onto the battlefield to taunt them? They were quaking in their sandals, safely behind friendly lines. Then a skinny sheepherder boy boldly steps forward, throws a single stone, killing the giant. Then he cuts off Goliath's head with the giant's own sword, probably to be sure the giant was really dead. God's plan all along, and talked about for thousands of years afterwards. There are many scriptures that reference and describe God's involvement in fighting (Psalm 33:16–17; Proverb 21:31; Zech 4:6).

Because, once again, it is all about our pride, which God is opposed to at a fundamental level.

He (God) *does not delight in the strength of the horse; he does not take pleasure in the legs of a man. The LORD favors those who faithfully respect Him, Those who wait for his loving kindness* (Psalm 147:10-11, NAS).

Speaking of the church, and how it functions in the world, Paul said:

The weapons we fight with are not the weapons of the world. On the contrary, they have divine power to demolish strongholds (2 Cor 10:4, also Ephesians 6:11-17).

We read in Revelation 19 that Jesus, riding a white horse, leads the armies of heaven, also riding on white horses; apparently, flying through the air to the earth. Is it possible, however remote, that the delay in the return of Jesus is so that the armies of heaven can be rebuilt, reconstituted, after the ejection of Satan and a third of the angels? So that when the final battle comes, the side of Good has an overwhelming numerical advantage. Not just to defeat Satan and his forces, but to also then have the power to throw them into the Abyss and keep them there for one thousand years (Isaiah 24:21-23; Rev 20:1-2).

What weapons do these armies carry? We do not know, but this is no pleasure ride. I do not know why we see less technology in reference to the heavenly forces: the angels seem to use only swords, and perhaps spears, and bows with arrows. I would be quite comfortable in a white flying sixty-ton US Army Abrams tank with a 120-millimeter smoothbore cannon on the front and coaxially mounted machine gun. Just point me in the right direction—tell me the plan, show me where to go—and my crew and I will do our part. Those we do not shoot will certainly get squashed.

So although the starship might have a military purpose and agenda, and knowing that the practical and experienced armies of heaven will probably be on board, we do not fly into a war zone based on the size of our ship, or our strength and past accomplishments. We maneuver and fight according to the will of God and his perfect plan for every tactical and strategic situation.

CONGRESS OF THE UNIVERSE

Armies may be necessary. However, just the arrival of the great starship may be enough to solve any crisis. *"Blessed are the peacemakers, for they will be called the children of God,"* (Matt 5:9).

Teddy Roosevelt said, "Walk softly and carry a big stick" (which he attributed to a West African proverb). I have also wondered if there would be a peacekeeping mission: fits the ship's name. Once the universe is at peace, the ship would visit planets or be available should a crisis develop somewhere. As people spread across the universe, the ship may be necessary to ensure a lasting peace and cooperation between worlds, races, and species.

In that light, the great ship could also serve as the site for a Congress of the Universe or Congress Interstellar. People would meet or live there and talk about issues of mutual concern like commerce, trade, colonization, immigration, communication, transportation, disease control, conflict mitigation, and more.

If Satan is not stirring up the delegates with pride, arrogance, and deception (because he is permanently imprisoned in the Abyss), imagine how fruitful and beneficial such a body would be. The hand of compassion would drive debates with mutual trust, hope, and love behind all negotiations, settlements, and outcomes.

CRUISE SHIP

Many Christians believe this immense cube-shaped object is a sort of everlasting luxury liner for believers, their reward for a life of faith. For them, the New Jerusalem is another word for heaven. If that is its purpose, perhaps it would work as a home base, and the immortal believers would live on the ship or on New Earth, as they chose, or by assignment.

The Bible does not say that the New Jerusalem spaceship is heaven. We read, *"The ship came down OUT OF heaven"* (Rev 21:2). This is an important distinction. The concept of the New Jerusalem being heaven itself minimizes its significance.

Personally, I would not be thrilled to find out that the spaceship or even the earth was supposed to be the only future heavenly abode. I would feel cheated somehow—shortchanged. Having said that, the Bible says God is transferring his flag—place of residence and operation—from the spiritual heaven to the ship for a period of time (Rev 21:3).

What exactly is going on? Why does God want to be on this ship—in this floating city?

And I heard a loud voice from the throne saying, "Now the dwelling of God is with people, and he will live with them." They will be his people, and God himself will be with them and be their God (Rev 21:3).

The original Greek of this passage reads:

Out of the throne, behold, the tabernacle of God is with people, and he will tabernacle with them. They shall be his people, and he shall be God with them, their God.

Let me tell you why this translation matters.

The distinction between *dwell* and *tabernacle* is important for the New Jerusalem, and *dwell* is a poor translation.

The word *dwell* means God will simply be in the city, residing there, like most of us. The other translation brings to mind the Old Testament allusion to the Tent of Meeting and the Holy of Holies where God's presence resided (Exodus 40:34-38). Do you remember the previous note about types and shadows? In the Tent of Meeting, Moses communed with God:

The LORD would speak to Moses face to face, as a man speaks with his friend (Exodus 33:11).

During the forty years in the wilderness, the Israelites looked up at the cloud of God's presence, hovering over the tabernacle—the Tent of Meeting, and knew God was there. Likewise, the people on New Earth will look to the heavens and see the New Jerusalem, and know God is near.

God will tabernacle with us, communing face to face: Reminds me of Adam walking with God in the cool of the evening. Everything is made right—even this. The restoration is complete—perfect union, perfect communion—profound in its love and simplicity.

However, the word *tabernacle*—a type of tent, brings a sense of the temporary. Would this transfer be permanent, or would there be a time when God returns to the spiritual realm—true heaven, which will still be there, or would he go somewhere else? When would that happen? More than a billion-trillion years could pass before he changes abode again, but use of the word *tabernacle* leaves me wondering about the timing. It could be that after a period of time, even the New Jerusalem might enter the spiritual realm, departing this universe, or go somewhere else, an entirely new place. Would that signal the end of eternity—this timeline, or the beginning of something new, or both?

So the real question is where do I want to be?

I want to be where God is, naturally, whether in the spiritual realm or on the spaceship in our physical universe. Being in his presence—the Essence of Absolute Love—is more important than where that actually happens. I want to walk with God in the cool of the evening, and like David, talk about what concerns him:

How precious to me are your thoughts, O God! How vast is the sum of them! (Psalm 139:17).

ARK

Could the New Jerusalem be an ark, seeding the habitable planets of the galaxy, perhaps even the universe? Not just with human life, but with all possible forms of life from the land, sea, and sky.

God is Creator. That is what he does. Then does God need an ark full of creatures? Probably not.

So I began to wonder if the ark concept would be a collaborative effort. He could take a planet and make it perfectly habitable, creating the perfect land and atmosphere, and plants and animals. Our job would be to manage the results, like Adam—shepherding and supervising.

Can you imagine if one or more levels of the New Jerusalem were like an aquarium, full of ocean life, with great depths and pressures necessary for some of the creatures? Another level might be a desert, teeming with the animals and insects peculiar to that climate. One whole level might be a tropical jungle, where afternoon rain showers nourish plants and animals. Another level could represent something like the Pacific Northwest with rainforests, a sea with orcas, mountain ranges, and cooler temperatures.

If not transplanted onto other planets, could the creatures be on the ark for our pleasure in oceans, deserts, arctic cold, forests, jungles, grasslands, and mountains: a rich diversity of life for the inhabitants to enjoy?

But what if the creatures on the ark represent intelligent species on other worlds? On one planet the highest form of intelligence might well reside in a lion species, or a race of eagles, or bull-like bovine herds: all able to communicate, express love and affection, create works of art, worship the Creator, and look to the heavens in wonder. There is a reason I chose these three.

A New Jerusalem ark, of course, reminds me of Noah.

Lots of Old Testament events were also allusions to or intimations—types and shadows—of New Testament events that occurred much later (see Heb 8:5, 9:23, 10:1). For example, Abraham attempting to sacrifice Isaac on Mount Moriah (Gen 22: The Akedah—The Binding of Isaac) was an allusion to the death of Jesus 2,000 years later on the same mountain, then called Golgotha. The Old Testament priestly system and office of the High Priest were allusions to events in the New Testament (see Heb 7:26-28).

The story of Noah might also be an Old Testament example of what was coming in the far distant future. Jerusalem means City of Peace, and the New Jerusalem could be the Ark of Peace, a great city, traveling through the galaxies.

STAR PRINCE AND STAR PRINCESS

Jesus said he would give his followers varying degrees of responsibility and some would be rulers. Rulers of what? Parts of the ship? Colonies? Planets? Solar systems? Galaxies? Would we be the new Star Princes and Star Princesses?

In the King James Version of the Bible, John 14:2, Jesus tells us:

In my Father's house are many mansions: if it were not so, I would have told you. I go to prepare a place for you.

The Greek word for "mansions," *monai,* also means "rooms," which could mean anything from a great castle to a New York apartment. But *monai* is better translated as "lodgings or dwellings." I think Jesus wanted to assure us that we would be with him (John 12:26, 14:3). Is Jesus referring to habitations in heaven, on New Earth, on the New Jerusalem, or something more fantastic? Hard to imagine, but with a starship parked in orbit and a universe to explore, anything is possible. So if Jesus is on the ship, and we are supposed to be with him, guess where you will be.

Before your imagination runs down the road of Star Princes and Star Princesses, *ruling solar systems,* study what God values first—God's leadership principles. Understand what kind of people God wants as leaders in his organization. The Bible gives us many examples, but start with Paul's letter to Titus: not arrogant, not violent, lover of good, self-controlled, holy, and disciplined. See also Paul's first letter to Timothy, chapters 3 and 4; and what Jesus said in Matt 20:25-28 and John 13:12-17. With God's help (perhaps only with God's help), we can become people he can really trust and use as future leaders. Simply put, in this life, we are in training to serve God and his plans for eternity, by serving and helping others. We are not here to see who avoids the most hardship and pain, or who pursues and gathers the most money, power, possessions, experiences, happiness, or pleasure. That is the world's view of life.

Jesus shared a parable about the resurrection—Matthew 25:31-46, one of my favorite passages in the Bible, and the surprise people felt when chosen. They did not realize that helping the hungry, the imprisoned, strangers, the destitute, and the sick would be of lasting value to God. But it is. It always is.

LEADERSHIP 101

Jesus told the parable of three people left in charge of an estate while the master was away (Matt 25:14-30). The master returned and told one who had increased the value, *"Well done, good and faithful servant! You have been faithful in a few things; I will put you in charge of many things. Come and share your master's happiness!"*

I can imagine different people left behind to govern and oversee the establishment of colonies and worlds throughout the universe. These rulers would probably have instantaneous communication with God and the ship, maybe even able to come and go between the planet and ship at will. By living on the ark, they would have gained practical knowledge of how to manage ecological systems and the various life forms associated with each. In that regard, the ark would be a great classroom.

LIFEBOAT

Timing is everything.

What I mean is that whatever purpose the New Jerusalem might have, when it first arrives at Earth, it is only a lifeboat. And that idea also fits with the story of Noah and his ark.

Look at how John starts Revelation chapter 21:

Then I saw a new heaven and a new earth, for the first heaven and first earth had passed away, and there was no longer any sea. I saw the Holy City, the New Jerusalem, coming down out of heaven from God.

Why a new earth?

With Satan's help and a great final war, we ruin the first earth. A final war so horrific, that even the oceans are destroyed, " . . . *no longer any sea.*" However, understanding what is going on can be confusing, because there are two great final wars described in the Bible during the End Times.

WORLD WAR III. The first great conflict culminates in the Valley of Armageddon, fifty-five miles *north* of Jerusalem.

WORLD WAR IV. The second battle, the last one that utterly destroys the world, concludes in the Valley of Jehoshaphat, just outside the walls of Jerusalem between the city and the Mount of Olives on the east side.

Isaiah, Ezekiel, Joel, Matthew, Luke, and Revelation mention the battle in the Valley of Armageddon. Most people are familiar with this battle from either the Bible or apocalyptic movies and documentaries. As Jesus arrives with the armies of heaven, Satan, the beast, the false prophet and their armies are defeated (Rev 19:19-21) and thrown into prison. Then Jesus rules the world from Jerusalem and the people experience 1,000 years of incredible peace.

But the prophet Joel in his short message and John in Revelation also speak of another battle, greater than the first, *after* the 1,000-year reign of Christ.

Why does this last war happen, if Jesus is ruling the world?

At the end of the 1,000-year reign of Christ, God allows Satan to depart or escape the Abyss prison. Satan deceives the nations—again, prodding and prompting them to destroy Jerusalem. Satan's maniacal rage and need for revenge knows no bounds. He not only wants to destroy Jerusalem, he wants Earth to be a smoking cinder block when he is done.

And it is.

The war that ends in the Valley of Jehoshaphat is so horrendous that God describes the scene as a Harvest of the Earth:

Let the nations be roused; let them advance into the Valley of Jehoshaphat, for there I will sit to judge all nations on every side. Swing the sickle, for the harvest is ripe. Come, trample the grapes, for the winepress is full and the vats overflow—so great is their wickedness! Multitudes, multitudes in the valley of decision! (Joel 3:12–14).

We read in Revelation chapter 20 that Satan puts together a new army, who surround the city of Jerusalem, " . . . *the city he* (God) *loves, but fire came down from heaven to devour them!*" (Rev 20:9). Here we need to go back and find Revelation 14:14–20, a short passage often titled in Bibles as *The Harvest of the Earth.* That section is out of sequence with everything else and easy to mistake where and when those events take place.

In this passage, the sickle also harvests a crop of people described as grapes:

The angel swung his sickle on the earth, gathering its grapes and threw them into the great winepress of God's wrath. They were trampled in the winepress outside the city, and the blood flowed out of the press, rising as high as the horses' bridles for a distance of 1,600 stadia (about 180 miles, Rev 14:19–20).

What weapon would reduce all living creatures to liquid, so that blood would rise four feet high, flowing from Jerusalem down to the Mediterranean Sea?

Enter the fluoro-antimonic bomb—also known as a FluBomb. A clear liquid acid so toxic it can liquefy glass—100 times more powerful than sulfuric acid. Despite the corrosiveness, it can be stored in simple PTFE—Teflon—containers. Exploded over a battlefield in great enough quantities, it would turn all exposed soldiers, animals, and most equipment into goo—a river of red. Mixed with burning fuel, it would be a horrific river of death, like the flow of magma from a volcano.

Microwave pulse weapons and focused radiation from a neutron bomb airburst incinerate humans, but also blood. Ultra sonic weapons can cause bones to explode, but these are focused weapons and would not necessarily cause the carnage described in the Bible. But give us 1,000 years to work on it, and who knows what else we can come up with.

Describing this event, the Apostle Peter said fire would lay bare the earth. Wiped clean.

The heavens will disappear with a roar. The elements will be destroyed by fire, and the earth and everything in it will be laid bare. But in keeping with his promise we are looking forward to a new heaven and a new earth (2 Peter 3:7, 10, 12-13).

Devastating, absolute destruction.

Isn't it interesting how Peter used the Greek word for *elements?* By using that specific word, Peter tells us that *everything* will be destroyed or contaminated beyond use, down to an elemental, basic level. Even if a bomb reduces some people to liquid outside the gates of Jerusalem, it sounds like old-fashioned nuclear weapons obliterate everything else on the planet at the end. Whatever humans contribute to the final outcome, it would not surprise me if God wiped the earth clean with a powerful solar flare. Why would he do that? If you are going to start over, you might as well take the old paint down to the metal before applying the new (Matt 9:17).

The Jews believed in multiple heavens, starting with the atmosphere, then outer space, and finally the spiritual plane. There are probably more levels beyond that. Paul said he was taken up into *the third heaven,* which would be the spiritual realm (2 Cor 12:2). So when God says he will create a new heaven and new earth, he actually means the planet Earth with its surrounding atmosphere. I can imagine God bringing some or all of the survivors into the New Jerusalem, during this period of re-creation—maybe for their own safety.

Apparently, God needs to wipe the slate clean and start over in order to create life on earth and make it ready for re-occupation. Only this time we will be in harmony with the earth, working together. We will look up and see the New Jerusalem in orbit, a constant reminder of our new reality. In addition, Satan will not be there to mess things up ever again.

Then I saw a new heaven and a new earth, for the first heaven and first earth had passed away . . . (Rev 21:1).

Passed away is an ominous phrase (ref. to people dying), but the Greek word *aperchomai* also means "to evaporate," vanish like vapor, while lasting a short time. Gone.

What happened? Before God placed the new heaven and new earth in place, he either caused the first earth and heaven to evaporate into nothingness, or he so completely reworked them, that they were unrecognizable, wiping the board utterly clean. A complete new beginning.

The simplest idea is that the old earth was spoiled and needed a radical makeover. What reality television shows would this re-creation event generate? Extreme Makeover Earth Edition, This Old Earth, Rip and Renew—Earth Version, Planet Hunters Renovation.

I get the impression that New Earth will be like a worldwide Garden of Eden, teeming with all kinds of life; perhaps all animals that were ever created and existed on the planet. Like at the beginning, a new explosion of life. Yes, I can imagine places where sauropods, hadrosaurs and stegosaurs roam freely, grazing alongside bison, giant sloths, and woolly mammoths.

Instead of hunting these amazing creatures into extinction—again, we will supervise and manage the results—hopefully living in simplicity and harmony. I am not even sure if we will still be meat eaters. There is a sense in Genesis that Adam and Eve were vegetarians before the Fall. Because when Adam and Eve sinned and required clothes, we read that God apparently killed animals for clothing: *"The LORD God made garments of skin . . ."* (Gen 3:21). After the family settled outside the Garden, we see seasonal animal sacrifices to God. Did God show Adam the right way to do an animal sacrifice? Did he then show Adam and Eve how to prepare the skins for clothing?

The Bible tells us that people on New Earth will visit the New Jerusalem. *"The kings of the earth will bring their splendor into it"* (Rev 21:24). Would we go to the airport and catch a shuttle, or could we just think about our destination and arrive on the Pearl Gate Platform of our choice?

With the introduction of anti-gravity, apparently a common system on the New Jerusalem that Earth could easily adopt (excitedly adopt), any properly outfitted vehicle could casually fly out of the atmosphere to the great starship without the violent thrust associated with rocket travel today.

Think about it: A world where anti-gravity is the norm in devices we can wear, vehicles we drive, and buildings we live in. Oceangoing ships would become obsolete, while someone like Disney Cruise Lines could offer tours out to Mars and the rings of Saturn during a long four-day weekend. Princess Cruises could fly down to Venus for fun, relaxation, and destination weddings. For nostalgic reasons, we might get on a real boat to go on an old-fashioned island-hopping cruise of the Caribbean.

We could live anywhere without the restrictions of obsolete roads and bridges. No more five o'clock rush hour traffic.

A new infrastructure would be required. Flying lanes would keep order and make travel as easy as speeding down our interstate highway or Autobahn system today. I can't wait.

But remember this: No matter how great life is on New Earth, there is still a starship parked in orbit above. However long it sits there, I am sure that someday it will travel to other places with a mission and purpose of its own.

Some scientists believe the universe is young, despite being 14 billion years old, and it would not be unusual for life to just now be appearing. In that light, we could be the Elder Race, the first people in the universe moving into space.

If life was not coursing through the universe already, God could begin a planet-by-planet creation event from the New Jerusalem. We cannot know at this time if we are the first planet with life, or one of many: I lean toward one of many, what with 100 billion planets just in our Milky Way. Are we the first planet with a redemption story, or one of many? Is it possible, however remotely, that what has happened here—the restoration of power and authority under Jesus Christ—allows us to go forward into the universe with something we did not have before: the power to be successful in whatever we take on, whatever corrections are required, whatever tasks are laid before us? That winning here would allow us to win everywhere, something not exactly true before

TRAVEL

CHAPTER FOUR

AND THE
UNIVERSE

MOVEMENT

Living on the ship, by definition, means we will have a destination, and I find this idea very exciting. Along that line, any object or place could have been used, not just a cube-shaped ship. God could have created or maneuvered a new moon into place for people to use, or even the minor planet Pluto. Instead, he chose to bring us a great ship. Not just any ship, but something built for travel in outer space—a spaceship, which by definition implies movement to another place—planets, stars, and galaxies in our universe.

God says he will live on this ship (Rev 21:3), which leads me to believe it will travel at the *speed of thought.*

What does it mean to travel at the speed of thought?

God would think of a place and the ship would just be there. In orbit. Instantaneously. The ship would not get there by moving really, really fast, using great engines to achieve great velocity, or warping space, or traveling rapidly through spiraling worm holes.

God created time and space with our universe—at least the time and space we know and try to understand, giving Stephen Hawking something to contemplate and write books about. This form of travel might work with God seeing or visualizing the location and we simply appear there.

MINDSHIFT

Think of it this way: God opens a window in the fabric of space (perhaps we can call it a worm window or worm door) using his mind. The window passes over—shifts, sort of swallowing the ship, which is not moving, and we find the ship in orbit around another planet. Or maybe the ship slowly passes or drifts through the window. On one side is our location, on the other side our destination.

Maybe we would stand at a great view screen. God would give us multiple location views and ask, "Where do you want to go today? The Horsehead Nebula? Great choice!"

MIND FOLD

Another idea is that God uses his mind to fold space, so that the destination will simply be next to the ship. Do this: Fold a piece of paper in half and punch a hole in it with something pointy—a pencil or pen. Now open the paper. Draw a straight line between these two points and label the hole on your left—A, your current location; label the hole on the right—B, your destination.

Now fold the paper again so the holes line up. Instead of traveling a great distance along the line you drew between points A and B, you just pass through the fold. The fold might pass over the ship, putting us in orbit around the new planet, or we might move or float past the fold into a new position above the next planet: similar to the Mind Shift but technically different.

CONCEPTION

For you *Star Trek* fans, God might have the ability to deconceive and reconceive us—deconception and reconception. We would cease to exist in one place and appear, literally recreated, at the destination—all of our molecules perfectly reassembled—no transcription errors. God holds all things together, so the idea that he could deconstruct and reconstruct something or someone is conceivable.

The conception idea comes from a verse in Colossians:

He is before all things, and in him all things hold together (Colossians 1:17).

Hold together. When I heard that scientists had discovered the fundamental particle—gluon—that holds all things together in the atom, I laughed, because I knew they were talking about God. Another name for God: the Glue that holds all things together. God Glue. When nothing else will hold . . .

God said, *"Do not I fill heaven and earth?"* (Jeremiah 23:24). He might have been talking about his spiritual presence, but he could also be describing his essential nature and essence: He fills it because he is it.

The implication is that one of the basic building blocks of the universe is gluons, and God is either gluons themselves—they are his essence (not just a part of his essence), or he is what makes gluons possible, something even smaller, basic, and elemental.

Note on quantum physics: Is there anything smaller than the electron, a basic and timeless particle? Photons, quarks, and weak vector bosons, like gluons, are basic and fundamental—each functioning in the realm of waves or particles, or both. So I was wondering if there was a more basic "thing" that formed the basic structure of these; perhaps something that actually exists in another dimension—the spiritual—while affecting this dimension and not readily measureable in our universe—which I am sure would make scientists grumpy. What's funny is that when physicists talk about what that basic "thing" might be, they are quick to add that it would also be absurdly powerful—Go GOD!

For transportation purposes, God would loosen the gluon bonding and we would cease to exist, floating painlessly apart, evaporating. His perfect memory would imagine us in another location where the gluons would reassemble perfectly. Wow! Takes the idea of trusting God to a whole new level!

GLUONS SIDENOTE

Gluons have a color charge—they have light—part of their composition, which in itself is interesting, because the Bible tells us *God is Light* (1 John 1:5). Quantum Chromodynamics is the science of this light. So when God says, *"Let there be light!"* in a sense he is commanding gluons to exist, scattered like glowing seeds across the universe, and do what they do, holding it all together while shining, everywhere.

Worm holes. Worm windows. Folding space. Deconception. It might be that if God thinks of the destination, we will just be there, and we will not know exactly how he did it until we are on board, and can ask.

Joel: *Excuse me. By the way, sir, how did you just do that, you know, moving instantly from our sun to Alpha Centauri?*

Jesus looks at me, smiling: *Come. Sit over here with us; I was just explaining that last movement to Stephen—*

The Bible describes this idea of a *window* between two points, two places—a fold in space or a worm window, touching, yet not actually next to each other.

In the parable about the Rich Man and Lazarus (Luke 16:19-31), Jesus describes a rich man suffering in hell. He wants a drink of water. Looking up, he sees Abraham far off and asks Abraham to send Lazarus with water to quench his unbearable thirst. Abraham explains that although they can see and talk to each other, there is *"a great chasm"* (verse 26) between them. Sounds like a two-way dimensional window, doesn't it? Reminds me of television—images I can see and hear but cannot move to: a great gulf separates me from the television station or source of transmission. Something like that is happening in the parable, suggesting how God might move the starship with his mind.

There is evidence of this instantaneous type of movement in the Gospel of John. Jesus had died and three days later rose from the dead. The disciples were in hiding behind locked doors for fear of discovery by the authorities. Suddenly, Jesus appeared among them, probably scared the wits out of the poor boys—not the normal come-and-go of the first century.

"Peace be with you!" Jesus said (John 20:19). Thomas was not there. Can we blame him for doubting?

Thomas comes by later, gives the secret knock on the door, and they let him in. Everyone is talking at once, exclaiming how Jesus appeared out of nowhere.

"Right," he says. "Just appeared over there by the table—whatever you say. And this, a room with a tiny second-floor window and two locked doors—ri - ght. You're messing with me again, aren't you guys? Well, I will not believe unless I can put my fingers into the holes in his hands and my hand into the wound in his side! Then I'll know you kidders didn't see a ghost!"

So what happens?

Jesus does it again—a week later, only this time Thomas is there.

Though the doors were locked, Jesus came and stood among them (John 20:26-28).

He tells Thomas to knock it off—to stop doubting and believe, which, of course, he does.

Jesus appeared suddenly among them—in a locked room. Just appeared. Isn't that what I am saying God can do with the New Jerusalem? Size differences would not thwart God.

The ability to move through space, appearing and disappearing, is a fascinating idea. I am wondering if this type of movement will be possible for all of us. Angels have wings for flying, while we teleport or apparate like Harry Potter, like Jesus. I am guessing that the ship could move in a similar fashion—however God does it.

In the end, the ship may be equipped with a mechanical system for traveling through the universe or dimensions, or for folding space—a type of engine or device that generates a special sub-space field. Either way, we will have to bring back Trans World Airlines.

When you get to Chapter 15, Alien Relatives: The Astronauts, I will explain how we might have relatives who are already adept at this form of travel.

THE DYNAMIC UNIVERSE

If we are going to explore the heavens, let me talk a little about the size and nature of the universe God has laid out for us to experience and enjoy—might make you appreciate the ship more.

The Bible does not exactly tell us what came before this universe, but we assume God dwelt in a spiritual realm already and sort of added our physical universe: inferred because he is there now and talks about having created everything here. The spiritual seems to exist either parallel, within, or contingent to our universe. But does the spiritual universe exist inside something else?—or parallel to something else?

It seems there was a previous creation of the spiritual dimension and the race of angels, because they rejoiced at the creation of our physical universe—Job 38:7, implying that God was even before that realm. I mean, where did God come from, if not another place, or object—before the spiritual—a first verse of a multi-verse series of creations? Although we may begin to roughly grasp where God might have come from, we will not know how until he tells us. Hopefully, at that time we will understand the answer.

LET THERE BE LIGHT

Many people assume the Bible begins with the creation event itself: *"Let there be light!"* (Gen 1:3), but it does not—note verse 3. The first two verses of the first chapter of Genesis start with a fairly odd description.

In the beginning God created the heavens and the earth. Now the earth was formless and empty, darkness was over the surface of the deep, and the Spirit of God was hovering over the waters (Gen 1:1-2).

What is going on here? Is this an overview or summarizing statement? Or is God telling us that the earth was a lifeless water or ice world made before absolutely anything else in our universe—before moons, planets, stars, and galaxies? I do not think either idea is accurate.

If you were a storyteller and wanted to set the stage for an astounding and extraordinary event, and your audience was mostly unlearned folk, you would need to keep the explanations and descriptions simple and understandable, at least as far as possible. When the first two verses mention heavens, earth, darkness, a deep, and waters, I wonder what else is going on. I am thinking about the earliest possible creation episode, couched in the simplest possible terminology. In other words, in the first two verses, God seems to be telling us, "This is what I started with."

Based on what I read in Genesis, I have always believed the universe was a bubble, mainly because I cannot imagine a universe without a boundary—just endless, openness. Then you can imagine my surprise when I found a scientific paper supporting what I had only imagined.[1]

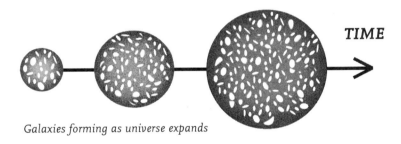

Galaxies forming as universe expands

Galaxies inside spherical closed energy system.
Permission: Tuomo: The Dynamic Universe.

The Bubble is a perfect expression of creation in its simplicity and purity of form: I am also thinking of the perfectly round pearl gates of the New Jerusalem. The idea of a bubble also implies that creation is three-dimensional, while the Bubble's interior would have four-dimensional properties in relation to space-time events and objects—think of the movie *Interstellar* and the black hole event horizon. We can surmise fourth-dimensional space outside the Bubble, but we cannot know or measure something like that at this time.

I believe the word *heavens*—the first object mentioned—speaks to the expanse of the Bubble, and is plural because it describes the stellar universe, *"stars of the heavens"* (Deuteronomy 10:22), and the idea of the parallel spiritual dimension at the same time—the third heaven of the scriptures (2 Cor 12:2—the first heaven our atmosphere, the second outer space).

The Hebrew word for earth is *erets* and means "dirt," dust, ground—rocks, and by extension land and countries. So it would be safe to say the word *earth* speaks to basic matter, all elements—not yet formed into anything—which are described as formless, void, empty, yet absolutely essential.

The Hebrew word for formless—without form—is *tohu* and has also been translated as "chaos and confusion." You cannot really say there is a planet present at this point in the story. The raw materials of *earth* are there, perhaps in a roiling round-shaped soup but with no sense of the size, before a Guiding Hand shapes and molds all of this matter into the desired order and harmony.

The Hebrew translation says, *"Darkness on the face of the deep."* The Hebrew word for *on* is often translated in Bibles as "over, covered, upon, or above." Interestingly, this word has also been used as "against or opposed." This led me to wonder if *darkness* was more than just darkness, or God's way of describing the presence of anti-matter and dark matter—against or opposed to matter—earth. Anti-matter and dark matter are not the same thing but necessary in the Creation event and outcome.

". . . on the face of the deep." Deep can be translated as "void," referring to a great empty place, the potential depths of creation, untapped, unrealized, essentially an empty, hollow bubble—or just the "face" of the Bubble, before it is anything. In fact, the Hebrew word *pawneem* often translated as "face" could be mouth, or presence of the *before*—a cryptic description. At this point in the story, the mouth of the Bubble could be flat. I am thinking of a wand dipped into the soap. The soap is flat on the wand until you blow and form the Bubble.

Elias David Graves blowing a bubble.

Deep sounds like an entity—perhaps electrons, which seems rather odd, unless it is a reference to the Bubble's nature—the potential state of things once the creation event starts; at the same time, the idea of surface tension in equilibrium in this pre-creation moment.

The Spirit—in Hebrew the RUAH or Breath of God (another reference to the soap bubble idea: blowing)—hovers over the waters, but scholars have translated it as brooding over the waters. This gives the scene a sense of expectation—appropriately, birth in waiting in an egg-shaped bubble. The RUAH is the hen brooding over creation, incubating her eggs, protecting them with her presence and warmth. Worrying over them. Pondering.

But I also think of RUAH as the energy aspect and character of the triune God—potential energy: in this case building up in zero entropy space.

God could not tell his readers that he started with oxygen and hydrogen, so what does he say? Water can be broken down into the basic elements of hydrogen and oxygen, which are key to the creation process. What will the RUAH Spirit and energy of God do with the hydrogen and oxygen? Simple: Create stars. Nuclear fusion powers stars when hydrogen turns into helium, giving us LIGHT, and stars create heavy elements (metals, nonmetals, semimetals), which we see represented as planets.

The stage is set with the necessary materials to begin creation.

RUAH broods until given the Word to Act. Darkness is in place over the Deep—the Bubble. Then, the RUAH—Breath of God, through the son of God, SPEAKS a WORD of intense and incredible energy into this perfect mix of formless matter—basic photons and gluons, antimatter, dark matter, elements of earth, hydrogen, oxygen, electrons—and creation begins. The Bubble forms.

God breathes the WORD, *LIGHT!* An extreme excitation of resting and potential energy is released. Gravitational and kinetic energy are borne in the outward motion following the LIGHT—energy, mass, momentum—from a zero energy balance and entropy to a higher entropy state. And the essential elements scatter across the expanding Bubble interior, not at the speed of light, rather each star purposefully positioned at the speed of God's mind. Enter velocity and gravity—mass as an expression of energy, including all forms of electromagnetic energy. Flowing and spinning outward, probably from a galactic center: Imagine ripples spreading outward in a pond, but that is mostly two-dimensional. Sound emanating from a tuning fork is a more accurate three-dimensional representation: sound flowing outward, everywhere. And sound brings the idea of perfect cosmic music, all parts, even what appears to be empty, resonating God's music—and God's mind.

The power present in this creation event, flowing from the RUAH, is beyond imagination. Look what happens when we split one atom—cities disappear. This power flows outward and begins to interact with its new environment: building blocks building, coursing through the universe—and our bodies.

The Apostle Paul knew something about this:

He is before all things, and in him all things hold together (Col 1:17).

God is Creator, and that means these substances and materials, these intricate parts of the creation event down to the level of gluons are God himself—at the elemental level—concentrated, unimaginable raw power. To me, that almost sounds scary. Righteous fear of the Lord might be a smart idea.

> *Fear of the LORD is the beginning of knowledge* (Proverbs 1:7). *Let all the earth fear the LORD* (Psalm 33:8).

Can you imagine, a God WHO IS every element in the universe, aware of every element in the universe—every part of his self, so that he even knows how many hairs are on your head at any given moment? That God would even take the time to consider such a mundane subject as my receding hairline. *"And even the very hairs on your head are numbered"* (Matt 10:30; Luke 12:7). A God WHO IS can say I AM.

Numbered?

The power of a single atom amazes us, but the sheer computational power of God is also beyond anything we can grasp or comprehend, even allowing us to have free will without compromising his predestined plans and eternal purposes. Which means God gives us a sense of ownership in the process, and the outcome. Yes, there is predestination, but our choices still matter. He tells us that over and over in the Bible: *"Choose this day who you will serve!"* (Joshua 24:15; 1 Kings 18:21).

Is THIS GOD big enough for you?

A creation event takes place in Genesis, and God is intricately and intimately involved. Still is.

Steven Weinberg said, "The more the universe seems comprehensible, the more it also seems pointless."[2]

I thought about Steven's statement a long time. Part of the answer is our basic need to find and know this God personally, to experience his love and then know he exists. I say this because God does want us to know his heart and mind. To understand at an intimate and personal level what David meant when he said, *"even when I go through tough times, you are with me"* (Ps 23:4, my translation).

The other part to Steven's statement takes us to the stand-off between science and faith and the need to find empirical evidence of God's fingerprints in creation—all of creation, from the micro to macro level, in how the universe works. I do not believe it is important to find a unifying theory for science and theology; we will not find commonality between the natural and supernatural. Scientists will study the natural universe and theologians will study God.

What I hope is that we will talk about the scientifically discoverable laws and processes that govern our world and the universe, and from the theological perspective find understanding, meaning, and purpose. In other words, we are studying the same thing, just from different perspectives, and both of those perspectives are valuable.

Saint Athanasius wrote, "He provided the works of creation also as a means by which the Maker might be known—Thus lay open to them, by which they might obtain the knowledge of God. They could look up into the immensity of heaven, and by pondering the harmony of creation come to know its Ruler, the Word of the Father, Whose all-ruling providence makes known the Father to all."[3]

A BIG BANG

It has been theorized that from any point in the universe, the universe will appear to be moving away from the observer. In that regard, the observable edge of the universe, at almost 14 billion light years away, may only reflect the limitations of our light gathering optics and nothing more. But Edwin Hubble's observations of the stars led him to postulate that they were moving away from us—our planet—expanding outward. Astronomers and physicists took this idea—working backwards—and theorized an explosive first or causal event—a big bang.

But based on my study of Genesis 1:1-2, it seems like a more "gentle" expression of creation was at work. No less powerful, by any means, but with stars spreading across the universe by the Breathed Word of God—the Trinitarian concept of RUAH, WORD, GOD—Elohim. Instead of an explosion emanating outward, we find a high-energy scattering and expansion, seeds thrown purposefully, deliberately, and consciously from the Sower's Hand—energy interacting with the basic building blocks, and the creation of NOW. TIME starts at a given point and cosmic time moves outward with gravitational energy and the energy of motion.

From this primal beginning, God created light and matter. Stars were born, lived, died, exploded, and reformed. As the stars reconstituted, basic elements in orbit coalesced into planets and the building blocks of life. We were created. So it would be safe to say we are made from stars. The First Breathing created stars and what became the dust of the ground, and a Second Breathing gave life to the first human.

And the LORD formed man of the dust of the ground, and breathed into his nostrils the breath of life and man became a living soul (Gen 2:7, KJV).

In college biology, we had to memorize and draw human cell and plant cell respiration. We learned that all life breathes in one fashion or another, which made me wonder if the universe breathes. Imagine galaxies circling the universe while exhibiting a three-dimensional (possibly also a four-dimensional) expansion, contraction, expansion, contraction model. God breathed into us and we began to breathe. Would it surprise you to learn that God breathed the universe into existence, and it continues to breathe also?

Think about it: If the universe is "alive," a living musical composition from and in the mind of God, then you would expect a type of respiration and metabolism, an exchange of gasses and material, to be ongoing. This would keep the universe "young" and dynamic, creating new stars from old, and it might explain the purpose of such things as black holes, shuffling material from one part of the universe to another, perhaps from an area where it is needed less, to an area where it is needed more—naturally.

From that causal beginning and into the present, nearly all objects rotate—the sun, planets, moons, stars, and galaxies. Stars rotate around the galactic center, and the galaxies probably rotate around the cosmic center of the Bubble. The farthest objects appear to be moving away, when in fact they might also be moving sideways or even away from each other in relation to our own position and movement around our galaxy, and the Milky Way galaxy's own movement and rotation in the universe. If the furthest light we can observe has traveled almost 14 billion light years, we could assume some kind of sidereal movement across that distance and time, while allowing for other influences, like from gravity.

The name of God—I AM, is God saying I EXIST or I AM EXISTENCE, also understood as NOW. I AM—NOW. As the author of creation and the substance of the creation event, he is the TIMELESS. In this respect, time moves in both directions for God. God can say I AM the Alpha and the Omega—the Beginning and the End (Rev 1:8, 22:13), seeing the end from the beginning (Isaiah 46:9-10), linking and holding everything together—timelessly. In this sense, God is saying I AM the Universe. The name he gave Moses, I AM, is most appropriate (Exodus 3:14). He can say, "Because I AM, YOU ARE—all things ARE, existing in the NOW."

In a 2008 *Discovery Magazine* article, Adam Frank said, "It is almost as if our universe were fine-tuned to start out far from equilibrium so it could possess an arrow of time. But to a physicist, invoking fine-tuning is akin to saying 'a miracle occurred.' For Carroll (Sean Carroll—theoretical physicist at Caltech), the challenge was finding a process that would explain the universe's low entropy naturally, without any appeal to incredible coincidence or (worse) to a miracle."[4]

CREATION DAYS REARRANGED

Let me finish this section with some thoughts on the first few days of the creation event. Genesis 1:16 says:

God made two great lights—the greater light to govern the day and the lesser light to govern the night. He also made the stars.

What is their purpose—the sun, moon, and these stars? The next verse says, *"God set them in the expanse of the sky* to give light to the earth." I have walked in the Mojave Desert on a moonless night, yet able to see my shadow and walk confidently without a flashlight by the light of the stars and the Milky Way brightly shining above.

How many stars can we actually see in the night sky? How many stars actually *"give light to the earth"* as described here in Genesis 1:17, so bright a person can see clearly? With the human eye, we can see about 2,500 to 3,200 stars shining on the earth on any given night.

Genesis 1:3—Day One, God calls into existence Light and Darkness. I have always assumed this meant the creation of galaxies, but when we get to Day Four, he creates the sun, the moon, *and the local stars,* who are all close enough to give Earth their light, so I can see my shadow by them.

Do not argue that God put the light in place, so that it did not need to travel—he does not work that way. If anything, God follows the set laws of physics and is methodical and precise: The life of Jesus is an excellent example—no shortcuts. I have heard people say, with a straight face, that God put the dinosaur bones in the ground—pre-aged, and the creatures never actually lived. What? That was the only way they could explain an 8,500-year-old Earth.

SUMMARY

DAY ZERO
Prep day, basic elements present but formless
(Gen 1:1-2)

DAY ONE
Use of basic elements to create Light and Dark—the creation of galaxies
(Gen 1:3-5)

DAY TWO
Creation of a water world (Earth) with sky or atmosphere
(Gen 1:6-8)

DAY THREE
Dry land appears out of the water, which brings forth vegetation
(Gen 1:9-13)

DAY FOUR
Creation of the sun, moon, and local stars
(Gen 1:14-19)

Is something out of place here? Don't plants and trees need the sun for warmth and nourishment? Could God create plants and trees on Day Three before there was a sun to sustain them on Day Four? I suppose, but not likely.

One theory is that the plants were actually primitive algae and did not necessarily need light. That would be like planting your vegetation in a deep freezer at absolute zero. Besides, the account clearly says seed-bearing plants and trees. They were alive and required light and warmth.

Would it be sacrilegious to suggest that one of the oldest stories ever told might need a little rearranging?

Move Day Four so it follows Day One, becoming the new Day Two. Then Light is created on Day One, on Day Two our local sun, moon, and nearby stars. On Day Three the water world called Earth appears with intact atmosphere. On Day Four dry land appears along with vegetation of all kinds. Now a plausible sequential creation is in place with everything ready for the explosion of life on the land and in the seas.

This would not be the first time that verses in the Bible were in the wrong place chronologically when finally written down. For example, Revelation 14:14-20—the Harvest of the Earth—is about the great final war *after* the 1,000-year reign of Jesus Christ at the end of all things. For continuity, this passage should follow Revelation 20:10.

Does all of this discussion about when things were created matter?

Some of you will say it does not matter because they believe the story is Christian mythology. Others will not care one way or the other. A third group will call my tampering heretical. But this is one of those subjects that gets fifth graders asking difficult questions.

What do you tell them?—plants did not need the sun for growth? That idea flies in the face of everything they are learning about the importance of the sun and the nature of plants. Do you tell them to stay quiet and take the passage on faith? I hope not, for a number of reasons, but it is often the default position for adults dealing with difficult questions from kids—or other adults.

Instead, ask them how they would rearrange events in the first chapter of Genesis. With a little study, some of them might put Day Four right after Day One—the new Day Two—because Earth needs the sun to be a liquid (versus ice) water world, from which land appears. Then tell them you know someone who agrees with this arrangement!

THE

CHAPTER FIVE

BUILDERS

WHO BUILT THE NEW JERUSALEM?

If God could create the whole universe and the amazing complexities of life down to the sub-atomic level, he could easily create a simple spaceship, even if it is the size of a small moon or Pluto. But did God create every piece of the ship or just the basic framework—walls, gates, foundation levels? Were angels involved somewhere in all of this? God gave us—humans—the ability to use our minds and create things from our imagination—the simple to the terrifying.

So I've wondered if people who have died—now in heaven—might be working on projects like this. What? Did you think the people who have died would be flitting around on white clouds, playing harps in celestial leisure? Don't be mistaken: Heaven is not Sarasota, Florida, the ultimate retirement location, where people lay on the beach, play shuffleboard, golf, and catch up on their reading (I know this is a slight exaggeration of retirement). In heaven, there are tasks to perform, things to learn, and purpose—divine purpose. Some people who have visited heaven (via visions and near-death experiences) report that some angels go around armed with swords. In the book of Revelation, John describes armies: They must train at some time.

Why would God need our help with the ship? Does God need help with anything? Would he still be omnipotent—all powerful, if he needs help or assistance from frail, flawed human beings like us?

Where humans are concerned, our relationship with God has always been collaborative—a partnership. We are even referred to as ambassadors of God's Message (2 Cor 5:20). God did not tell Adam what to call the animals; he gave Adam the task of naming them. Instead of waving his hand and making the Tabernacle and Holy of Holies appear, God blessed people with the ability to be great craftpersons.

And he has filled him with the Spirit of God, with skill, with intelligence, with knowledge, and with all craftsmanship, to devise artistic designs, to work in gold and silver and bronze (Exodus 35:31-32, 35).

We all have gifts and talents, which God intends for us to use to accomplish his purposes in the Church, our lives, relationships, and occupations, then in heaven. Would that change because we went to heaven or boarded a starship? Of course not.

Consider the Parable of the Talents (Matt 25:14–30). The master leaves three servants to look after his estate while he is away. Upon his return, he learns two servants have worked hard and used their talents to increase the value. He is pleased. In fact, there is a sense from the passage that he is highly pleased—with exclamations—and tells each:

Well done, good and faithful servant! You have been faithful with a few things; I will put you in charge of many things. Come and share your master's happiness (verse 23).

I have always understood this parable to mean that Jesus is the Master, who leaves for a long time. The servants are the people who work for him in his absence, who then die and go to heaven. We can be diligent about our duties and responsibilities or lazy bums. This parable implies that the life spent in faith and service to God, obeying his Word while helping and serving others, will be rewarded with some kind of leadership role in heaven.

LEADERSHIP ROLES

Like the 115-mile-high levels in the New Jerusalem, I am convinced that the whole universe is not a big waste of space. There is a reason for its size. It has a purpose, and its size is not a hindering factor, but rather necessary in ways we cannot comprehend at this time. There are trillions of galaxies. Perhaps the whole universe will be our new Garden of Eden with people assigned to supervise star systems—Earth always as the home world. Adam had dominion over the earth, and I believe we will have dominion over the stars.

Another issue I find interesting is that God must have furnished the raw materials, and perhaps most of the finished products for building the spaceship. The ship is so big that we could not build it with all the resources of Earth. Just the size and weight would mean it could not be built on the surface of a large planet. Someone built the New Jerusalem in space.

I have already stretched your imagination a little, so when I suggest that there might be a spaceport construction and maintenance facility producing these starships, would you be surprised? The New Jerusalem is probably complete and standing by, but why would it be the only cube-shaped starship *in the fleet?*

At the time I was writing this, a news article appeared about the strange dimming of star KIC 8462852. NASA's Kepler space telescope has been watching stars from orbit since 2009. When a star dims slightly, that indicates a possible planet transit, crossing between us and the distant star—an eclipse. How much the star dims tells us the relative size of the planet in orbit.

But at KIC 8462852, 1,480 light years away in the constellation of Cygnus the Swan, something is causing the star to dim by fifteen and twenty percent—at *random* intervals, not predictable like ordinary planetary orbits. Unheard of.

Let me give some perspective.

If you were on a planet almost 1,500 light years away from our sun and our largest planet, Jupiter, crossed in front of your space telescope, the light would dim by only one percent. Then you would have to wait twelve years to see Jupiter pass by again, dimming one percent with each transit—a *predictable* interval based on the planet's predictable orbit. You would learn things about Jupiter each time—size, atmosphere, surface temperatures, direction of spin, and orbit.

Whatever this is at star KIC 8462852, it is big, immense, and the star dims *unpredictably* by fifteen to twenty percent.

Possible scientific explanations for this intermittent dimming include: A swarm of comets and their debris, or extremely large planets orbiting on different planes. The star itself might not be round due to an extremely fast rotation, causing all kinds of gravitational anomalies with emerging light variations. Something like Jupiter's great spot, but on the star, could disrupt light as its unusual spin brings the object into and out of our view. The star might be notably dim but have a relatively bright spot that rotates in and out of view. Lots of possibilities.

However, at this time, scientists have ruled out the "scientific" explanations, leaving people to wonder if an alien super structure of some kind is blocking the light.[1]

If you are building thousands of starships in space, each 1,380 miles to a side (some could be much larger), you could be blocking significant portions of a star's light. In addition, if the ships are made of crystal, all kinds of light diffraction and reflection issues could be at play, disrupting the Kepler telescope's view. With crystal spaceships, Kepler would see the light from the spaceport itself, as it reflects its own starlight back to us, similar to how the moon reflects our sun's light, causing or exasperating the random and unpredictable readings.

If the spaceport were closer to us, the disruption of light would be more profound. I mean, if you hold a golf ball up in front of your eye, it will effectively block the sun better than if it is one hundred feet away. So the space station would have more of a blocking effect if further out from the star and closer to us.

If God can create the vast immensity of the universe, whose complexity and size staggers our minds and imaginations, he could easily create a fleet of these ships—of all sizes.

Why would God create a fleet of ships?

How big is the universe? How many galaxies are in this universe? Beyond count. Is this the only universe? Are there others? There are many possible reasons to produce a fleet of ships. It is also feasible that other species of intelligent creatures will have their own ships.

As we learn about the universe's needs and God's plans, the requirement for all of these ships, who will pilot what, and the variety of destinations will become clear.

Do you think God will let us call one of these starships the *Enterprise*?

STAR SHIP

CHAPTER SIX

ARRIVAL

THE BIBLE TELLS US WHEN THE NEW JERUSALEM WILL ARRIVE

Discussion about the universe and speculation on the place and purpose of a starship like this falls into the realm of cosmology (okay, and probably a little science fiction and fantasy—science prophecy). Studies of the Bible to determine *when* the ship will arrive moves us into the area of eschatology (eska-tology: in the Greek *éschatos* means "last"), the theological study of last things—the End Times.

In Revelation 19:11 John describes Jesus the Warrior returning to Earth:

There before me was a white horse, whose rider is called Faithful and True. With justice he makes war—the armies of heaven were following him.

This event is the Second Coming—the First Coming being his birth, life, crucifixion, and resurrection more than 2,000 years ago. With the armies of heaven, Jesus defeats the Beast (a.k.a. the anti-Christ)—Satan's puppet. God's angels throw Satan and his henchmen into the Abyss, and Jesus rules the world from his throne in Jerusalem for 1,000 years. Worldwide peace follows—a world without Satan or his diabolical influence.

At the end of Jesus' 1,000-year reign, God allows Satan to leave the Abyss prison. He quickly deceives the people of Earth—again, who attack Jerusalem. At that time, the New Jerusalem spaceship arrives.

So the advent of the New Jerusalem—the starship's arrival in orbit around Earth—hinges on the Second Coming of Jesus. If the Second Coming event is hundreds of years from now, or longer, why waste time wondering or talking about it here?

Because the return of Jesus is imminent—soon.
This is why this story has relevancy today.

Jesus said he would come back:

For the Son of Man is going to come in his Father's glory with his angels . . . (Matt 16:27, 24:37-39, and others).

But skeptics remind us that for thousands of years people have been saying the return of Jesus to Earth would happen in their lifetime.

In the Apostle Peter's first letter, he wrote:

The end of all things is near (1 Peter 4:7).

James, the brother of Jesus, wrote:

You too, be patient and stand firm, because the Lord's coming is near (James 5:8).

The author of Hebrews thought Jesus could come back at any time:

Let us not give up meeting together, as some are in the habit of doing, but let us encourage one another—and all the more as you see the Day approaching (Heb 10:25).

Martin Luther of the Reformation (1483–1546) believed he was in the End Times, because he thought the Catholic papacy represented Satan undermining Christendom. All through the ages, we have heard about groups of people, proclaiming that the return of Jesus was about to happen—in their lifetime—and nothing. As they sold everything and waited on hilltops—some for alien spaceships, we referred to them as delusional lunatics, cults, or evil sects.

If all of this is true and everyone got it wrong, why would I venture out on that unstable limb to suggest that the Second Coming must be in the near future? Because one event has happened that had not happened before—until now.

In the Gospel of Luke, we read that Jesus was teaching in the Great Temple. He might have been a little annoyed: While he was trying to explain the practice of giving sacrificially, the disciples' attention seems to be elsewhere, *"... remarking about how the temple was adorned with beautiful stones"* (Luke 21:5).

Herod the Great—governor of Judea, that brutal and paranoid character, who butchered the children of Bethlehem while searching for the baby Jesus (Matt 2:16-18, Massacre of the Innocents)—took on a great and ambitious building project, perhaps the largest construction endeavor in the Roman Empire at the time. Herod was keen to leave behind monumental legacies of his kingship.

One gem in his architectural belt was a massive expansion of the Great Temple—The Second Temple. The first temple built by Solomon (1 Kings 6) was destroyed by the Babylonians in 586 BC and rebuilt after the seventy-year Jewish exile in Babylon (see Dan 9:1–2; Ezra 1:1–4; 2 Chronicles 36:22-23).

Herod's work was a marvel of the time with parts of the interior covered in gold—in particular, the Holy of Holies. Some of the stones supporting the outer wall were 44 feet by 11 feet by 16 feet, weighing up to 628 tons. The average stone in the complex weighed in at 28 tons; a truly monumental wonder of the Roman world.

In John 2:19–21, Jesus was in the Great Temple, speaking to the Pharisees about himself, and said:

Destroy this temple (actually referring to his body) *and I will raise it again in three days.' Not understanding him, the Pharisees cried, "It has taken forty-six years to build this temple, and you are going to raise it in three days?"*

Forty-six years. Massive and ornate. Built to astonish the viewer, but Jesus was not impressed. As he looked around at the building, I'm sure he frowned while waving his hand about, and saying:

As for what you see here, the time will come when not one stone will be left on another; every one of them will be thrown down (Luke 21:6; Matt 24:2).

The disciples were shocked. They asked each other how could the immense blocks be toppled and the temple destroyed? The Gospel of Matthew tells us they all retired to the Mount of Olives, down the hill from Jerusalem and across the valley.

When settled in the garden, the disciples asked Jesus a two-part question:

When will these things happen? And what will be the sign that they are about to take place? (Luke 21:7).

TIMING AND SIGNS

Jesus starts with the signs, describing the end of the world, earthquakes, famine, harbingers in the heavens, the persecution of believers, and Jerusalem surrounded by armies: a time of desperation and suffering.

However, to answer the question about timing, he tells a parable:

Look at the fig tree and all of the trees. When they sprout leaves, you can see for yourselves and know that summer is near. Even so, when you see these things happening, you know that the kingdom of God is near (Luke 21:29–31; Matt 24:32–33).

We know from other scriptures that the fig tree is a metaphor for Israel (Fig tree: Matt 21:18–20; Mark 11:12–14; Luke 13:6–9; Habakkuk 3:17–18; Jeremiah 24:4–7). Jesus tells his disciples the new growth and sprouting leaves of the fig tree will be a sign for the timing. What does that sign look like? What has happened with Israel and Jerusalem in particular?

A HISTORY LESSON

Who had Jerusalem when Jesus was here? The Romans—Gentiles, non-Jews. Do you remember the Roman Prefect—Pontius Pilate, washing his hands after the trial of Jesus? At that time, some people were hoping Jesus was a warrior Messiah (Gen 49:10; Isaiah 13:4–5, 24:21–23; Ezek 7:27; Joel 2:11) who would lead mighty armies to drive out the oppressors, then appoint them as leaders. Judas Iscariot thought like that, but Jesus had other plans. (The Old Testament mentions both Messiahs: the humble servant and the conquering warrior).

Then in 70 AD, as Jesus predicted, Emperor Titus and General Tiberius, leading four legions of Roman soldiers, destroyed Jerusalem and the Great Temple. Only the retaining walls that supported the Temple above remain, one portion of which is the well-known Wailing Wall. As Jesus said, the Romans tore the temple apart to get the gold that melted down between the stone seams, and the Israelites scattered for their lives to settle in other nations—the Diaspora.

The Prophet Ezekiel predicted this event more than 500 years before—about 586 BC. He quoted God as saying:

I dispersed them among the nations, and they were scattered through the countries; I judged them according to their conduct and their actions (Ezek 36:19).

Although many Jewish people had been leaving Israel and not coming back for hundreds of years, this event caused most of the remaining Jews to leave. For rejecting their Messiah, God cursed the fig tree, which withered.

Ezekiel predicted or prophesied the Diaspora, but he also said God would bring the Jewish people back to their own land:

Then they will know that I am the LORD their God, for though I sent them into exile among the nations, I will gather them to their own land, not leaving any behind (Ezek 39:28; 37:12, 21).

Ezekiel tells us that this will happen, *"In future years"* (Ezek 38:8, *"In latter years"* KJV).

Israel becoming a nation after thousands of years is the fig tree sprouting tender shoots and leaves, becoming a beautiful tree again: a specific sign for us.

Jesus gave another important sign, saying that the Gentiles would control Jerusalem for a precise period.

"Jerusalem will be trampled on by the Gentiles until the times of the Gentiles are fulfilled" (Luke 21:24).

What does that mean, *". . . the times of the Gentiles fulfilled?"*

From the time of Jesus until the end of World War II, Gentiles controlled Jerusalem—the time of the Gentiles. In 1948, the nation of Israel was born, and the Jews gained control over half of Jerusalem, but they did not govern the whole city. All of Jerusalem finally came under their jurisdiction after the Six-Day War in 1967.

Although many people throughout the ages thought Jesus might come sooner, incorrectly predicting his return, this part of the prophecy did not happen until now—*in our lifetime.* With all of Jerusalem under Jewish control for the first time in 2,000 plus years, the time of the Gentiles was fulfilled—complete: another specific sign for us.

"When will these things happen?"

It is all about the timing.

PART ONE
Israel becomes a nation.

PART TWO
The Jews control all of Jerusalem.

Is it any wonder that the Jewish people are adamantly opposed to a divided Jerusalem? The Palestinians want Jerusalem as their capitol also, but dividing Jerusalem is simply not negotiable.

When all of Jerusalem came under Jewish control, the final sign presented itself and the clock started ticking down. Jesus said:

I tell you the truth, this generation will certainly not pass away until all these things have happened (Matt 24:34; Luke 21:32).

A GENERATION

What does that passage mean, and how does it affect us? We need to know how long a generation is.

From the time of King David until now, the general lifespan of an individual has been about seventy years.

The length of our days is seventy years—or eighty, if we have the strength (Psalm 90:10).

Despite the advances of science over the centuries, from birth to death the *lifespan* of a generation is still approximately seventy years. Because of hardship, *life expectancy* can vary in certain countries today as in times past. Do you see the distinction between lifespan and life expectancy? Likewise, in biblical times, those people with access to plentiful food and good medical care, like kings, could live a long life.

Even 2,700 years ago, this was true:

At that time Tyre will be forgotten for seventy years, the span of a king's life. (Isaiah 23:15, who lived in the 700s BC).

In modern countries with ready access to medical care and an abundance of quality, clean food and water, life expectancy has slowly crept up into the low eighties. However, that does not change the truth spoken of in Psalm 90, of what the average lifespan is supposed to be—seventy years.

So add seventy years—the average length of a generation from birth to death—to the date 1967 when all of Jerusalem was captured, and we have Jesus returning to Earth *before the year 2037*. He said he would return *before* that generation passed away, who witnessed a specific event: all of Jerusalem controlled by the Jews. He said it was a certainty—take it to the bank. This means that *most of you reading this will witness his return!*

Now notice, I did not give you a specific date and ask you to sell your possessions, climb a mountain with me, and beat drums while chanting Kumbaya. No. What we have is a range. Jesus will return *before* 2037, and that date is not far off, is it?

As Jesus said, we will not know the exact date and time, which is just as well. *"But about that day or hour no one knows, not even the angels in heaven, nor the Son, but only the Father"* (Matt 24:36). Knowing he will return between now and 2037 should be enough to motivate into action everyone who believes.

Are you beginning to feel a sense of urgency?
I certainly do.

DELIBERATION 1

What happens if Jesus does not come back by 2037? Psalm 90:10 did allow for eighty years: *"The length of our days is seventy years—or eighty,"* making the return *before* 2047.

DELIBERATION 2

The year 2037 is the seventy-year span of a "standard" generation, but what if God is watching certain individuals or a person, who would live longer? This idea came from Simeon:

> *Now there was a man in Jerusalem called Simeon, who was righteous and devout. He was waiting for the consolation of Israel, and the Holy Spirit was on him. It had been revealed to him by the Holy Spirit that he would not die before he had seen the Lord's Messiah* (Lk 1:25–26).

While we can expect the return of Jesus before 2037, God can choose one individual of that generation as the one to watch, *however long they live*. Imagine Grandma Johnson—of our generation—living 96 years and God uses her lifespan to launch the Second Coming—26 years later—2063. I would be disappointed. I often pray for Jesus to come quickly and end this world's misery. And I would like to still be alive for the Second Coming—to be transformed in the wink of an eye (1 Cor 15:52).

DELIBERATION 3

Here's an unusual twist: Isn't it interesting that Dr. Neil DeGrasse describes a great asteroid striking the United States in the Midwest some time in 2036? What if the following scripture speaks to this horrific event:

> *The third angel sounded his trumpet and a great star, blazing like a torch, fell from the sky . . . the name of the star is Wormwood* (Rev 8:10-11).

Wormwood is about calamity, suffering, and grief. Neil calls the asteroid Apophis, the Egyptian god of chaos and darkness—how appropriate. If Apophis is the mountain of Revelation 8, then this collision of earth and rock takes place in the last half of the seven-year Great Tribulation. That means the Second Coming would be *before* 2040.

God has a plan, and although I have ideas about when certain things will happen, the End Time events will unfold in the fullness of time and not a second earlier—or later.

THE
CHAPTER SEVEN
WAR

ALIENS AT WAR—
HUMANS IN THE MIDDLE

Think about it: The Bible says Jesus comes back just in time to save the human race from total annihilation—extinction (Matt 24:22). The great ship arrives at Earth because we are coming to the end of a long and difficult conflict, culminating in a great final battle on the steps of Jerusalem: a horrific battle in the Valley of Jehoshaphat at the end of all things (Joel 3:2, 12).

Why does this happen? Why are there two great wars—World War III and World War IV?—worse by far than the previous two world wars, worse than all wars combined.

We have a sense of something wrong, pending, looming—what I call a build-up of spiritual negative energy. Before the 2004 tsunami hit Indonesia, many pets and animals fled to high ground. The ocean retreated from the shore while a few people ventured out onto the expanding beach to collect seashells, completely unaware—but not everyone.

Like the animals, we sense something: Impending doom? Imminent disaster? Foreboding? I have talked to people who have had dystopian dreams—nightmares of post-apocalyptic survival during or after a profound disaster. I have had them. Fighting to survive. Enduring hardship and suffering. Everywhere. Loved ones in trouble. Trying to escape something, an aggressor, a disaster, famine.

"The world is demonstrably worse than when I started—have I caused this?" asked Jon Stewart, American comedian, departing from his show in August 2015. No, you did not cause it, but everyone notices how the world seems to be sick and failing on multiple levels.

There is an exponential increase in fighting, terrorism, rumors of war, military build-ups, wrongful land grabs, deceit, the changing moral and ethical fabric all around the world, psychotic behaviors, gossip, pride, cruelty, arrogance, revenge, gross violence, mass shootings, false accusations, greater addictions to alcohol, drugs, porn, gambling, video sub-realities—and fear.

Lots of fear.

Fear seems to be predominant, pervasive. Fear is oxygen for terrorists, bullies, anarchists, predators, and those seeking to impose their will on the helpless, or those who dare resist them. Real and perceived victim fear gives the terrorist or leader life and purpose, and for some the way they rule. These are all acts of control by force, but also wretchedly pathetic manipulation.

When I was a kid, we ran around the neighborhood all day and stumbled into the house at dinnertime, often after dark. Few people now let their kids out of sight for so long.

Life is not particularly safe anymore. When a family allows their kids to travel or walk alone in the city or play unsupervised in a local park (free-range parenting), anxious neighbors call the police or Child Protective Services (CPS), and the parents are accused of being irresponsible, negligent, or worse. The parents naturally and sincerely want their kids to learn something important: self-reliance, independence, the fun of adventures, but all everyone else sees is danger.

Where is the danger coming from?

Every day, all around the world, we hear about human predation, slavery, radicalisms, extremisms, immense hubris, angers, cruelties, horrors, and senseless violence. Few things damage the soul like pornography. Gross violence in films and video games hurt people, inside, at a basic level: sort of desensitizing the soul and numbing the mind to what should be horror. A certain level of rage seems to permeate societies at every level, in every country. While the family is the foundation of any society, divorce and domestic/relational violence are rampant across demographics.

As I write this, 2015, in Charleston, South Carolina, a young man massacred nine people attending a bible study at Emanuel African Methodist Episcopal Church. In Norway, 2011, Anders Breivik killed 77 people and complained that he could not kill more. In America, we will always remember September 11, 2001. Terrorists attacked Paris in November 2015, killing 130 people and injuring many others. And then we have the massacre in Orlando, Florida.

Threats from radical Islam and other extremist groups keep everyone on edge, while Iran tries to build The Bomb and North Korea threatens to use it. Massacres in churches and holy institutions around the world mean sacred places are not respected or the people worshiping there. Some of what used to be R-rated on television and the movies is now PG-13. I watch for the specific sub-rating of gross violence as a way of avoiding such films.

Mass shootings have become commonplace in the United States, motivated by anger, hate, and mental illness. I am especially troubled by parents killing their children. As gun sales and gun thefts soar, more "lone wolf" attacks will come, with many people senselessly killed. New extremist groups will appear, while the old ones feel reenergized.

From now on, it will only get worse.

I am sorry to bring you this news; I am sad and very sorry. But you already know all this, don't you? It is discouraging. This is the End Times World we live in—Satan's cesspool. The Bible tells us that in the End Times:

Because of the increase in wickedness, the love of most will grow cold (Matt 24:12).

Love growing cold implies withdrawal (or denial) as a personal protection defense mechanism and desensitization to the violence: a mental and emotional numbness to what we experience and how we respond. Violence fatigue. Depression.

The evening news reporter lamented that school shootings were becoming commonplace. In recent years, I have noticed an uptick in the incidents of people attacking school-aged children *around the world*. In places where guns are not permitted or prevalent, they attack young children in schools using knives and other sharp instruments: sociopaths and the mentally unstable attacking the most vulnerable.

That is why people see the danger in young ones out alone in our societies— everywhere. Therefore, it is time to stop the free-range parenting experiment in your home; it is an irresponsible and terrible gamble with your child's safety and life in this present world.

WHY IS ALL OF THIS HAPPENING?

As a hospice chaplain, I learned that there is always a spiritual aspect to the physical and emotional pain people suffer, and the physical violence in the world has a spiritual basis also.

In the spiritual realm, the balance of power on Earth is shifting rapidly and actively into Satan's control. An ongoing war in another dimension is spilling over into our world and intensifying as we near the end of this age. Those few people who are not mentally stable become key players in this battle—for the enemy. Those who take drugs, make themselves mentally unstable, pawns for his potential control.

The Miami Police Department warned its patrol officers that the bath salt designer drug—Cloud 9—was causing people to act like they were demon-possessed, with zombie-like, flesh-eating attacks on people. Act like it? Who is to say that by taking this drug, they had willingly, or unwillingly, invited demon possession with all of its horrifying ramifications?

As these global existential pains increase, we see a continuous and pervasive lack of honor, shame, guilt, contrition, mercy, and grace. While the world's moral compass spins around out of control, we are being overwhelmed by wickedness and evil. So would you be surprised to learn that exorcisms are up all around the world?

Let me elaborate.

The Bible tells us that the spiritual universe existed long before what we call our physical universe. It may be that the spiritual universe is just another type of physical universe, or a parallel universe in another dimension. However, for simplicity and clarity, I will refer to the place where God and angels dwell as the spiritual, and the place where we live on Earth as the physical, although vigorous and scientific (or theological) debates might allow for other, or overlapping, ideas.

The Bible implies that our universe followed the other because God purposely, at a given moment, created this physical universe—bound by space and time—as described in Genesis chapter 1 and the Gospel of John chapter 1. He started somewhere else, adding this universe, created from scratch, outside of the place where he was, and is.

This further suggests that the problem on Earth—the war-like state we are all experiencing now—started *before* the creation of our universe. I would even go so far as to suggest that the creation of this new physical universe, and in particular Earth and humans—in anticipation of our Fall and redemption story—was integral to a Great Plan to correct the problem caused by the rebellion of Satan with his angels, if that is the only problem.

What does the following verse mean?

All inhabitants of the earth will worship the Beast—all whose names have not been written in the book of life belonging to the Lamb that was slain from the creation of the world (Rev 13:8).

Actually, in the Greek, this verse says "Slain from the founding of the cosmos."

This means that at the dawn of our universe's creation, the requirement for the incarnation of God as a human called Jesus Christ, and the death and resurrection of Jesus to redeem fallen humans and defeat Satan, was already in their plans.

Peter said it this way:

He (Jesus) was chosen before the creation of the world, but was revealed in these last times for your sake (1 Peter 1:20).

Why did that happen?

At some time in the distant past, there was a wreck. The rebellion of Satan seriously upset or damaged something—perhaps the balance of power and authority, probably because he became the anti-God, anti-love, the absolute polar opposite—opposed to all God stands for and represents. Satan wanted to rule all creation—not because he was gifted or talented that way, but because he believed it was his right, his destiny, his purpose. And if he could not get it all, he would at least muck up the realm, and what we might call the human story. Full of pride and arrogance, lacking any semblance of empathy, he thinks he has the ability to bring it all down and corrupt everything.

But God anticipated this—from the beginning.

Because Jesus was successful in his mission, we read:

And God placed all things under his feet and appointed him to be the head over everything for the church . . . (Eph 1:22).

This implies that *everything* was NOT exactly under his feet or under his control before his sinless life and successful death and resurrection. Remember, I said that the problem began *before* God created our universe.

For he has put everything under his feet. Now when it says that 'everything' has been put under him, it is clear that this does not include God himself, who put everything under Christ (1 Cor 15:27, also Philippians 2:5-11).

The letter to the Hebrews expands upon what Paul just described in 1 Corinthians. The subjection of all creation—the physical and spiritual universes—under Jesus' feet is not complete—yet.

You have put all things in subjection under his feet. For in that he put all in subjection under him, he left nothing that is not put under him. But now we see not yet all things put under him (Heb 2:8).

This passage is talking about the promise and the fulfillment that follows. There is a sense that it is an ongoing process and a timing issue.

For us, the spiritual war has been raging from Genesis chapter one, is happening now, and will not be over until the end of the Book of Revelation. That is one of the Bible's predominant themes throughout.

Back to the story.

The war in heaven spilled over into our present timeline when humans in the Garden disobeyed God, and that disobedience damaged their relationship with God. Many changes took place at that time, but let me talk about two.

First, while humans lived in the Garden, life was as perfect as it could get. But when they disobeyed God, our many problems began: death, diseases, hurts, fears, pains, horrors, pride, and arrogance to name a few.

So when someone says they cannot believe in God because he lets bad things happen to good people, back up a second. We chose. We told God we could manage our lives better without his aide or interference. The Bible is really all about the failure in the Garden, the resulting Fall, and necessary redemption of humans. Eve had two boys, and what happened right out of the chute? Cain kills Abel! Hasn't it been like that ever since? And we are the only ones to blame.

Second, Satan seems to have received some level of power and authority from the Fall of humans, because we read that after Jesus died and rose from the dead, he—Jesus—got something back that he didn't previously have: the Keys to Death.

Did you ever wonder why Jesus descended into hell after he died on the cross? He took the fight into Satan's realm for the first time. He was on a quest, a mission, to get something back that had been lost. And he could get there no other way.

DUNGEONS

What is hell? Is it a real place or made up?

The Prophet Zechariah wrote about the Messiah's Triumphal Entry into Jerusalem:

Rejoice greatly, O daughter of Zion! Shout, daughter of Jerusalem! See, your King comes to you, righteous and having salvation, gentle and riding on a donkey, on a colt, the foal of a donkey (Zech 9:9, the Humble Messiah).

Then, a few verses later, he announces that this person, the Messiah who brings Salvation, will free those in hell.

As for you, because of the blood of my covenant with you, I will free your prisoners from the waterless pit (Zech 9:11).

People do not believe in hell for many reasons:

1. Some do not believe in hell because they cannot wrap their minds around an eternity of suffering. They cannot imagine a place of eternal punishment because God is love (1 John 4:8) and should not tolerate such an outcome. "If God is so good, how can he make a hell, much less throw people into it?" In their minds, the God who would create a hell to punish people for eternity, just for rejecting him, is not a God worth worshiping.

2. Some do not believe in hell because as intellectually efficient and superior beings, they feel more informed and enlightened than primitive or provincial believers, and write off all of the hell notions as Christian mythology and delusion. Some of these same people believe in heaven.

3. I had a relative tell me, firmly, that hell was our life on earth, and heaven was whatever happened afterwards, which had to be better than this mess.

4. Finally, some people believe heaven and hell are real, but only in our minds: not actual real places.

The Old Testament mentions hell as we just read and Jesus talked about hell, so the argument that it was a later invention of the Middle Ages is patently false.

Hell. This word captures a lot of meaning in the English language, while in the Bible it means different things. The Apostle John referred to a *"fiery lake of burning sulfur"* (Rev 21:8). Jesus called it a place of *"eternal punishment"* (Matt 25:46). David said, *"The wicked return to the grave . . ."* (Psalm 9:17). In a parable, Jesus said the angels:

> *Throw them (evil people) into the fiery furnace . . .* (Matt 13:50). *Then he will say to those on his left, "Depart from me, you who are cursed, into the eternal fire prepared for the devil and his angels"* (Matt 25:41; 2 Peter 2:4). *They will be punished with everlasting destruction and shut out from the presence of the LORD . . .* (2 Thessalonians 1:9).

That, I think, speaks to the essence of hell—*being shut out from God*. Separated.

Here's the rub: God is love. People with pride, arrogance, condescension, and pretension (which includes most of us) cannot stand before him unless he sees them through the blood of Jesus (think red filter), so those people who reject him have to go somewhere after death. Wherever that is, it will be separation from God—shut out from God. Eternity is a long time. I have wondered if there will be second chances for those who come to their senses late, reference Jesus preaching to the spirits in prison: something to wonder about, but not something to gamble on.

We read that Satan got the key to a bottomless pit, but we also read that he had the Key to Death—are they the same? For a time, he seemed to be able to capture the souls of the dead, holding them in a special place, deep in the earth. We also read that there is a region referred to as the Abyss. Demons do not want to go there, and it might be a place where certain angels wait in chains for the final judgment. At the Second Coming of Jesus, we read that Satan, the Beast, the False Prophet and their followers are thrown into the Abyss. If you believe in heaven, then believe in this necessary place. Jesus did not actually speak of hell more than heaven, but he did speak of the place, and it sounds scary.

WEEPING AND GNASHING
OF TEETH

Jesus speaks of two places that we would describe as hell: The Lake of Fire (a.k.a. Blazing Furnace), that place we are all familiar with from stories, sermons, and movies, where there will be weeping and gnashing of teeth. And there is another place equally unpleasant—Outer Darkness, where there will be weeping and gnashing of teeth (Matt 8:12, 13:42, 50, 22:13).

I was on the operating table one time (Anaheim General about 1974) and felt every cut of the surgeon's knife—excision of a pilonidal cyst. I grasped the headboard bars with all my strength, while nurses held me down. One nurse rolled up a towel and stuck it between my teeth. I screamed repeatedly; I mean *screamed!*—weeping-and-gnashing-of-teeth type of anguish. The surgeon kept saying he was almost done—for five minutes. I passed out, waking up in the ICU. So I can tell you with some authority and experience that weeping and gnashing of teeth is not something you want to experience for any length of time.

I can imagine why the Lake of Fire would be hellish, but what about the Outer Darkness? There might be something about that region we do not fully grasp. Does despair, regret, fear, and anguish feel overwhelming, producing a sense of existential pain? While the furnace is a place of intense heat, unquenched thirst and all that implies, is Outer Darkness about intense, bitter, bone-gnawing cold with no relief or hope?—a cold that cuts like a knife? Could Outer Darkness be outside the Bubble of this creation or in another dimension? Who would choose either option—hot or cold?—in either case, an immortal soul lost.

I saw a star fallen from heaven to earth, and he was given the key to the shaft of the bottomless pit (Rev 9:1, ESV).

Look out: Satan got the key to the dungeon!

"*And he was given . . .*" The Greek for that verse is *edoth* or "given," but is better translated as "permitted or granted." I have pointed this out to be sure you understand that God only allows Satan to do certain things, and for events to happen the way they do for reasons only he really knows. He is God after all, the Alpha and the Omega, who sees the end from the beginning (Isaiah 46:9-11; Rev 21:6). This is where we get the idea of omniscience—knowing all things. He has an outcome in mind, which we perceive dimly in the scriptures. Sometimes we complain that we do not like his methods or some of the outcomes: ants railing against the rain. The Book of Job is a good example of what I am trying to explain here. By some accounts, Job might be the oldest book in the Bible.

"*Have you considered my servant Job?*" God asked Satan (Job 1:8).

God brings up the subject and grants Satan permission to do certain things to Job within defined limits. This conversation has always bothered me—an odd exchange. God is sort of pulling Satan into the story, who admits he had had such thoughts, but knew his hands were tied or restricted, with boundaries he must operate within.

The story is about how Satan did all kinds of horrible things to Job, but Job kept his faith in God. Could this Job story be a metaphor for our overall post-Fall human condition?—with Satan trying to get as many humans as possible to reject God, one way or another? Just might be—figuratively and literally.

Before you completely reject this notion of God pulling someone into a story against their will, look at Ezekiel 38. Gog of Magog of the far north (who I believe is Russia) did not intend to attack Israel, but God said:

> I will turn you around, put hooks in your jaws and bring you out with your whole army. You will advance against my people Israel like a cloud that covers the land. In days to come, O Gog, I will bring you against my land, so that the nations may know me when I show myself holy through you before their eyes (Ezek 38:4, 16).

In Ezekiel chapters 36 and 37, Israel becomes a nation again, which we talked about. I believe Ezekiel 38 through 39 are about World War III—the great battle in the Valley of Armageddon, known as the Valley of Hamon Gog during Ezekiel's time (Ezek 39:11). If you ever wondered why all of this is going to happen, here is the answer: *God's purpose is to show his holiness before the nations.*

God has a purpose.

He uses Gog of Magog, and he uses Satan to get the outcome he desires. He permits things to happen, which would happen anyhow if the Holy Spirit did not constantly restrain Satan (2 Thess 2:7). In other words, at times, God lessens and weakens the restraints, and Satan does what he planned to do all along.

God would not permit Satan to kill Job, but in the End Times, all restraints finally fall away, and he lets Satan have the *"power to make war against the saints* (believers) *and to conquer them"* (Rev 13:7). We must be at peace with this scripture, rest assured, knowing God is in control, holy, and has a specific outcome and result in mind: something that could not be accomplished any other way (Lk 22:42). If anything, God is efficient, and we must learn to trust him explicitly. If God calls you to martyrdom—conquered and dying for your faith, know in your heart and mind that God is with you and this is a great honor. Peter said it this way:

> But if anyone suffers as a Christian, they are not to be ashamed, but are to glorify God in this name (1 Peter 4:16).

Then there is a parable called *The Rich Man and Lazarus* (Luke 16:19-31). The rich man and the poor man die. The rich man, unnamed, finds himself in a lake of fire, while the poor man, Lazarus, is with Father Abraham, in a place called Abraham's Bosom—the resting place of the righteous dead.

In Greek, the word for "bosom" is *kolpos,* meaning "lap." When someone reclined for a meal in the first century Middle East, seated near the host, they were in the bosom of the host. We know that after his death, Jesus descended into hell, yet he told the thief on the cross he would be with him *that day in Paradise* (Luke 23:43). Then is Paradise hell?

Just a parable, right? But study closely and you begin to see something interesting.

People who died *before* the resurrection of Jesus, it seems, did not go directly to heaven, that spiritual realm where God is, which we would expect. Instead, they were caught in a middle place, waiting. Jesus called it Paradise. Abraham's Bosom was Paradise.

Note: This is not purgatory. Purgatory comes from a Roman Catholic teaching of a place where people are purged of venial sins—minor sins, before they are allowed into heaven. They must atone for their own sins through penance—voluntary self-punishment, because God's grace—through the shed blood of Jesus Christ—is not sufficient. This purgatory doctrine is patently false—not in the Bible—and flies in the face of 1 Peter 3:18:

For Christ died for sins once for all, the righteous for the unrighteous, to bring you to God.

There is no salvation merit in our personal efforts and works: We cannot save ourselves or atone for our own sins—venial or otherwise—period. See also Ephesians 2:8–9.

In another passage, we learn that these people in Paradise are captives. Jesus went there to share something—speaking to certain people, and after three days, he led those held captive out of the dungeon to heaven. At that time, I believe Paradise either ceased to exist, or became just another part of hell—sort of filled in. If Guantanamo Bay military prison closed, it would automatically become part of Cuba again.

When you ascended on high, you took many captives . . . (Psalm 68:18).

Peter explains it this way:

After being made alive, he went and made proclamation to the imprisoned spirits, to those who were disobedient long ago when God waited patiently in the days of Noah while the ark was being built (1 Peter 3:19-20).

Jesus spoke to the spirits, but we do not know exactly who they are or what he said. Would God give the people of Noah's time another chance to believe because they did not understand what was taking place—the destruction of their world in the flood? Why does Peter single out these people as imprisoned and not others? Could it be that people who died prior to the appearance of Abraham were actually "imprisoned," while others experienced something different with the arrival of Abraham—Paradise? So that would mean there were three regions of hell: the Lake of Fire, another place where certain spirits are or were imprisoned in chains, and Abraham's Bosom.

The Apostle Paul wrote:

And he (God) made known to us his good pleasure, which he purposed in Christ, to be put into effect when the times will have reached their fulfillment—to bring all things in heaven and on earth together under one head, even Christ (Eph 1:9-10).

God's plan is to restore everything, to put back into order the system broken by the rebellion of Satan. This is not really a contest to see who wins. Rather, it has been and is a methodical and simple plan: one that will result in a new creation and the restoration of God's kingdom in both dimensions—spiritual and physical.

His (God's) intent was that now, through the Church, the manifold wisdom of God should be made known to the rulers and authorities in the heavenly realms (Eph 3:10).

Doesn't that statement sound somewhat galactic? *"The rulers and authorities in the heavenly realms . . ."*

Sometimes I get the feeling that a lot more has been at stake than we can imagine. And how could we imagine? We are in the middle of this crisis, suffering and dying, loving and hoping, all while being fully centered on ourselves: feeling blessed by God one minute, then shaking our fist at him in rage, anger, and frustration the next, because something went wrong in our lives, or someone we loved got sick or died. We shout, "IF YOU ARE SO BIG AND SO SMART AND SO LOVING, WHY DID MY PRECIOUS CHILD DIE!?"

How can we fully comprehend these events, or everything that is threatened or in jeopardy, when all we really and truly care about is ourselves and our loved ones? Nearly impossible. Mostly impossible. We cannot comprehend our own temporary life picture, much less God's cosmic magnum opus. That is one reason I wrote this: so we could study the clues and delve into this a little deeper to discover what is going on, and what our role(s) might be.

Rulers and authorities in the heavenly realms.

Realms—plural. Are there galactic empires watching, waiting? Are there participants or observers on the sidelines, waiting for the outcome *of this particular conflict* to decide what they will do—or not do? How far does Satan's rebellion actually stretch? Heavenly realms? How vast and extensive does this term "realms" encompass? Do you remember my comment about Star Princes? Are they watching this conflict to decide how to go forward?—capitulate or fight?

But to each one of us grace has been given as Christ apportioned it. This is why it says: "When he ascended on high, he took many captives and gave gifts to his people." What does "he ascended" mean except that he also descended to the lower, earthly regions? He who descended is the very one who ascended higher than all the heavens, in order to fill the whole universe (Ephesians 4:7–10).

Here is another cosmic statement from the Apostle Paul. *". . . all the heavens—in order to fill the whole universe."*

Makes me think of the starship and the possible uses God might have for it—and us. The whole universe will be filled, and I am thinking it will be a process we are intimately involved in over an eternity. Do you realize how big *the whole universe* is?—beyond our imagination. The whole *Star Wars* saga takes place in one galaxy, and there are trillions of galaxies in our universe.

We understand from this next verse that Satan fell to Earth with a third of the angels. His angels, apparently. But what else is going on here?

And another sign appeared in heaven: and behold, a great red dragon having seven heads and ten horns, and on his heads were seven diadems. And his tail swept away a third of the stars of heaven, and threw them to the earth (Revelation 12:3–4).

The people writing these stories and letters that ended up in the Bible knew a lot about what was really going on. They had visions and dreams, writing down what they saw, while trying to explain things in a language we could understand, at least partially. It might also be that they were not given all of the answers themselves or all of the information at one time, and we have received everything they had—incomplete or baffling as it is; baffling even for some of them.

For example, the angel specifically told John not to reveal what he learned from the Seven Thunders (Rev 10:4). Both Daniel (Dan 7:16) and John (Rev 7:13-14; 17:6-18) had to have things they saw explained to them by angels, but even the answers can leave us scratching our heads.

SUMMARY

Jesus went to hell (also called *sheol* in the Hebrew, *hades* in the Greek), and spoke to the spirits of certain angels and people who had died. After three days, he freed people trapped in Paradise, leading them to heaven. I am not sure if Jesus freed those in chains. By his life, death, and resurrection, he corrected previous wrongs and set the stage for a universal restoration.

I am guessing that when Satan won in the Garden and God expelled Adam and Eve, this was one of the things he gained, somehow: the ability to capture and hold souls in his spiritual domain from the time of Adam until the death of Jesus. Satan controlled the keys to Death and Hades.

Because Jesus brings us comfort by announcing:

Do not be afraid. I am the First and the Last. I am the Living One. I was dead, and behold I am alive forever and ever! And I hold the keys to Death and Hades (Rev 1:17-18).

Rejoice! Now Jesus has the keys!

Jesus was victorious, but do you sense in these words a militaristic aspect to all of this? Even if he did not free the Jews from their Roman oppressors as the military leader they expected, he was a humble and obedient *soldier* nevertheless. Phil 2:8, "*He was obedient unto death.*" Jesus was in a deadly contest with the devil, because Satan was always looking for an opportunity to trip him up, causing him to fail in his mission (Luke 4:13).

Since that time (his death and resurrection) *he* (Jesus) *waits for his enemies to be made his footstool* . . . (Heb 10:13).

As I said before, whatever was gained is not complete at this time. Jesus is waiting. We are waiting. The war is ongoing.

The broken relationship with God, starting with the Fall of humans, had to be repaired—somehow—or Satan would be the winner. Because of rules set in place before the foundation of the world—probably before our universe existed—the only possible solution was for God himself, to fix the problem. But isn't that what I have been saying? He knew there would be a wreck and appointed himself as the solution, within the established constraints, because we could not fix it ourselves. And we certainly could not fix what was previously broken.

BECAUSE OF RULES

Rules are important. God cannot casually appear at the mall and perform miracles to convince people of who he is and his purposes. For one thing, his absolute lack of pride forbids it. Instead, he talks to us through nature, the Bible, prayer, dreams and visions, and other people, so we can discover the answers for ourselves. He gave us the ability to be successful in this task by filling us with an internal yearning for meaning and purpose in our lives, felt by all people around the world. He tells us that if we believe in him, he will place his Spirit inside us, so we can call him *Daddy* (*Abba*) and be effective as his children (Romans 8:14-17), living in this fallen world.

Ezekiel predicted this:

I will give you a new heart and a new spirit in you; I will remove from you your heart of stone and give you a heart of flesh. And (and this is important, explaining why) *I will put my Spirit in you and move you to follow my decrees and be careful about keeping my laws* (Ezek 36:26-27).

In other words, God would help us to be successful in this ongoing conflict.

Ezekiel was a prophet and said this would happen in the future. Did it come true? Jesus told his disciples that after he returned to the Father, he would then send the Spirit. So this becomes another benefit for us of the resurrection.

Unless I go away, the Counselor (the Holy Spirit) *will not come to you; but if I go, I will send him to you* (John 16:7, 14:23-27).

What difference does this make, receiving the Spirit?

I want to say it is all about power, but that sounds like something the world would value and exploit. The Holy Spirit does give real spiritual power, but I find that the Spirit also gives knowledge, which itself is a form of power. The Spirit has different names, based on our needs. In my NIV Bible, John 14:16 describes the Spirit of God as a

Counselor, but the Greek of that word, *parakleton,* is better translated as "Comforter, Helper, Advocate, Personal Trainer, Tutor." I mean, if we decide to stand for God against the world, wouldn't it be nice to have a little help, a little comfort, guidance, training—a little power?

Because of the ancient rules, God uses us to be his face and voice to a world at war, bringing help, hope, and redemption—face to face, with people in need. Not the smartest idea in my mind: using us?—flawed, broken, miserable, wretched human beings? It is like trying to win a fight with your left arm tied behind your back, standing on one leg, while blindfolded. Satan must have jumped at the chance to enter that ring.

For example, the most powerful person to ever enter our world was God incarnate, Jesus, with God before and at the creation of our universe. He humbled himself, renouncing the personal use of all power for his own benefit—*and he wins.* Some might think it a great tragedy that Jesus died in his early thirties, but it was a great victory all around, because he obeyed God explicitly, strictly, only doing exactly what his Father told him to do, saying only what his Father told him to say, and absolutely nothing else. Period. Crazy.

And being found in appearance as a man, he humbled himself and became obedient to death—even death on a cross! (Phil 2:8).

He did not live his own life; he lived the life God outlined for him in order to be victorious. You might say the end justified the means. We would be quick to criticize anyone acting like that now, while others might call them saints.

That is also why the Gnostic literature about Jesus is false and heretical. In those writings, like the Gospel of Thomas, the child Jesus uses his power for his own pleasure or purposes. Jesus would not give up his calling as Messiah to have an affair with Mary Magdalene, much less marry her and have children. Either of these would negate his calling, because he would be serving himself at the expense of humankind. I wonder what creature would benefit from promoting these kinds of stories—sowing doubt and confusion?

That is the essence of the incarnation—God became human. God became a human so he could enter our world and universe, perfectly fixing the problem himself, forever.

The New Testament is hidden in the Old, and the Old Testament is revealed in the New. For example, the Old Testament has many allusions to the incarnation, but my favorite is the Akedah—the Binding of Isaac, which I mentioned earlier. This event took place about 1,900 years before Christ. To make a long story short, God told Abraham to sacrifice his only son. A shocking idea; something practiced by the heathen nations around him. In strict obedience to God's command, Abraham and Isaac walked up Mount Moriah to perform the sad deed. Isaac carried the wood. As they prepared, Isaac—37 years old, asked his father, Abraham—137 years old, where was the sacrificial animal?

Abraham told his son:

God, himself, will provide the lamb for the burnt offering, my son (Gen 22:8).

The Sacrifice of Abraham by Rembrandt, 1635, The Hermitage, St. Petersburg, Russia. A play on words: Isaac is the one being sacrificed, so I would wonder that it should be called *The Sacrifice of Isaac*. But Abraham is performing the sacrifice in obedience to God, his sacrifice to God.

Isn't it interesting that this statement in the Hebrew could also be understood as, *"God will provide, himself, the lamb . . ."?*

Also in strict and absolute obedience to his father, this young man, who could have easily overwhelmed the old man, lay obediently on the altar built of rocks and sticks.

After Abraham's dire pronouncement, in my mind, I see them both weeping softly, neither speaking. Abraham goes about his grim task in hopes that God will bring his promised son back to life after he is dead (Heb 11:19): To Abraham, Isaac has already been dead during the three-day hike to the mountain. Isaac lies back on the pile of sticks, a desperate pleading in his eyes for understanding, yet trusting, as his father ties him down. He weeps in bewilderment, confusion, and as his father takes the wicked knife in hand, growing horror. He closes his eyes tightly, panting, and waits. Before Abraham could slay his son, an angel calls out to stop him, and they discover a goat conveniently wedged in a nearby bush.

Why did I tell you the Akedah story?

This disturbing story is only interesting if you learn later that Mount Moriah becomes known as Mount Calvary or Golgotha, where God incarnate—God *himself*—offered his only son almost 2,000 years later as the sacrificial lamb. He shed his human blood for the sins of the whole world, then went to hell for three days, before rising from the dead—figuratively like Isaac.

Speaking of Jesus, Isaiah wrote:

He was oppressed and afflicted, yet he did not open his mouth; he was led like a lamb to the slaughter, and as a sheep before her shearers is silent, so he did not open his mouth (Isaiah 53:7).

Isaac obediently lay down, and Abraham tied him to the pile of sticks; Jesus lay down and Roman soldiers nailed him to the cross, then stood it up for all to gaze upon. Isaac was the type and shadow of a promise and Jesus the fulfillment.

Only God could right the wrongs by becoming a human. In addition, he does not just fix the relationship problem between humans and himself, there is the restoration of his authority in certain spiritual areas, in the heavens and in the realms, with the whole universe affected. As I said, it is complicated. And magnificent.

Imagine that: A cosmic plan of restoration and reconciliation conceived and set in motion more than 13 billion years ago to correct a problem that developed in another universe, in another time. I use the figure 13 billion, because, at this time, that is the distance to the farthest object we can observe with a space telescope, as measured by the red shift distance light has traveled. Meaning the most distant galaxy we can observe, God created more than 13 billion years ago. Talk about a long-range strategic plan.

Sounds like a *Star Wars* epic space opera, a saga and historical drama of cosmic proportions. God, gods, villains, heroes, victims, oppressed people, mythical creatures, battles seen, unseen, and suspected: all of the elements that make up a great story, ending in a climatic battle, redemption of a fallen people, punishment of an ancient foe, with the hero, at the end, riding in on a white horse to save the day. Now you know where westerns got the idea.

This is an intricate and old story, and it is important to uncover the many facts and facets so we can understand what is happening, what is at stake, and what our roles and responsibilities might be *should we choose them.*

I want to present this idea of God coming to us from another perspective—as Lover. Here is a brief parable by philosopher Søren Kierkegaard presented by James Gettel. I find the reasonableness of the story to be compelling and understandable at a very basic level:

Once upon a time there lived a king who loved a poor maiden. The king was all-powerful in his land, and no one would dare prevent his marriage to whomever he pleased, despite differences in class. But the maiden did not know the king or suspect his love for her.

The king's love became a peculiar sort of tragedy. Because he desired the maiden and her true love and understanding, he could not approach his beloved as the king. For if he were to appear to the maiden as a king, she would be awed by the differences between them. She could worship and admire him for his power and status, but she could not forget that he was the king and that she was but a humble maiden. As a true lover, the king desired not to be glorified by the maiden, but to glorify her. He desired her true understanding and equality in love, and he knew true love could come only through his beloved's freedom, courage, and self-confidence. These all-important attributes of love would not blossom in the unequal relationship of king and subject. The differences between the king and the maiden would prevent either from being confident, understanding, or happy in their love.

The king considered the possibility of elevating the maiden to his equal through secret gifts, transfiguring her to the joys of being a princess. But he quickly realized the folly of this approach. If the maiden accepted her good fortune, their love would be only a delusion created by the king. And, if the maiden were not completely deluded, in her heart she would suspect the deception and thereby recognize the differences between herself and the king. In either case, the elevation would be catastrophic if it changed the character of the maiden. For the king loved her for herself! "It was harder for him to be her benefactor than to love her," for he knew that "love does not alter the beloved, it alters itself."

The king grieved. How could he help his beloved to understand him as he wished to be understood, as a lover rather than as a king? "For this is the unfathomable nature of love, that it desires equality with the beloved, not in jest merely, but in earnest and truth." If their union could not be effected through the maiden's elevation to the king, it must be attempted through the king's "descent" to the maiden. The king realized he had to "appear in the likeness of the humblest." He therefore had to appear as a servant, as one humbled enough to serve others. So he clothed himself in a beggar's cloak and went out to meet the maiden.[1]

Paul wrote about Jesus:

He made himself nothing by taking the very nature of a servant, being made in human likeness (Phil 2:7).

The person of Jesus is the king come to Earth, calling to each of us, personally, now, by the Holy Spirit, moving our heart to choose him. Every person who chooses Jesus is a maiden who finds her king with the promise of this relationship into all eternity.

Does this idea make you uncomfortable?—being referred to as a maiden in relation to the king or Jesus?

Like all things in the New Testament, it started in the Old Testament. Isaiah speaking to the land of Israel, said,

"For your Maker is your husband—the LORD Almighty is his name—the Holy One of Israel is your Redeemer; he is called the God of all the earth. The Lord will call you back as if you were a wife deserted and distressed in spirit—a wife who married young, only to be rejected," says your God (Isa 54:5-6).

Later Isaiah speaks about Jerusalem in the same language:

As a young man marries a young woman, so will your Builder marry you; as a bridegroom rejoices over his bride, so will your God rejoice over you (Isa 62:5).

So how does the Israel bride translate into the Church bride?

For one thing, Israel has not gone away, as Paul reminds us: Israel is the branch and we are grafted in (see Romans 11, Isa 5:1-7). But Galatians 3 tells us that we are children of Abraham by faith when we accept Christ.

So in Christ Jesus you are all children of God through faith, for all of you who were baptized into Christ have clothed yourselves with Christ. There is neither Jew nor Gentile, neither slave nor free, nor is there male and female, for you are all one in Christ Jesus. If you belong to Christ, then you are Abraham's seed, and heirs according to the promise (Gal 3:26-29).

In Matthew 22, Jesus tells the parable of the Wedding Banquet, implying that believers are the bride. Then in Matthew 25, he talks about the bridegroom coming unexpectedly, so everyone should watch carefully for his arrival. Paul understood this intimate relationship. Speaking to the Galatian church, he said:

I am jealous for you with a godly jealousy. I promised you to one husband, to Christ, so that I might present you as a pure virgin to him (2 Cor 11:2).

And then we come to Revelation 19. John witnesses a great multitude described as the bride of the Lamb (Jesus) and holy people.

Then I heard what sounded like a great multitude, like the roar of rushing waters and like loud peals of thunder, shouting: "Hallelujah!

For our Lord God Almighty reigns. Let us rejoice and be glad and give him glory! For the wedding of the Lamb has come, and his bride has made herself ready. Fine linen, bright and clean, was given her to wear."(Fine linen stands for the righteous acts of God's holy people.) Then the angel said to me, "Write this: Blessed are those who are invited to the wedding supper of the Lamb!" And he added, "These are the true words of God" (Rev 19:6–9).

So think of the Maiden in Søren's parable as another name for the Bride of Christ—all faithful believers, a metaphor that helps us understand the intimacy and importance of our relationship to Jesus and God, individually and corporately. That his love for us probably runs deeper and wider and stronger than we can ever truly and fully imagine in this life.

DEALING WITH FEAR

Before I close this section on war, I want to go back to fear. When terrorists and bullies attack (as represented by individuals, organizations, and countries), people are injured—physically, mentally, and spiritually. These attacks generate fear in the community. Society suffers an ongoing victimization because fear persists after the evil actions, often in anticipation of another or series of attacks, although not necessarily just where the violence took place. Like ripples on the pond from a stone, an attack on Paris is felt around the world, and other societies wonder if they will be targeted and harmed. The looming threat affects all.

Jesus talks about this. When he was here, people sought to kill him.

Peace I leave with you; my peace I give you. Not as the world gives do I give to you. Let not your hearts be troubled, neither let them be afraid (John 14:27).

The disciples hid in fear after Jesus died. Out of fear, Peter denied Him—repeatedly, but something changed. A short time later, Peter boldly stood in the crowded square and announced the Good News of Jesus Christ. When arrested, Peter and John assured the authorities that they would continue sharing about Jesus, whatever the threats. So what changed?

John wrote:

God lives in us and his love is made complete in us. God is love. There is no fear in love. But perfect love drives out fear (1 John 4:12, 16, 18).

David said that even if he had to walk a scary path, *"through the valley of the shadow of death, I will fear no evil, for you (God) are with me"* (Psalm 23:4).

The question then is how can we be sure God is with us and that we have the Peace of Jesus driving out fear, while causing us to remain calm, confident, and hopeful? John also said in this same passage:

> *This is how God showed his love among us: He sent his one and only Son into the world that we might live through him* (1 John 4:9).

We live without fear by *living through Jesus.* Trusting Him. During fearful times, pray and ask God to fill you with his Spirit of Love—the Peace of Jesus. In this way, fear is driven away from the inside out. Then, like the disciples, you will boldly go where once you cringed in fear.

> *Fear not, for I am with you; be not dismayed, for I am your God; I will strengthen you, I will help you, I will uphold you with my righteous right hand* (Isaiah 41:10).

During fearful times, pray and ask God to intervene in your heart, transforming you from the inside out. Then your fear will dissipate, and you will be able to comfort others with the comfort you have received.

THE

CHAPTER EIGHT

GARDEN

HOW DID THE WAR START?
FOR US, IT ALL BEGAN IN A GARDEN

God allowed Satan, using a lizard or dragon—what the Bible calls a serpent (the creature's punishment was to lose its legs, crawling on its belly), to enter the Garden and speak to the principle leaders. We do not know how long this conversation took place, but I am guessing he worked on them over an extremely long time. Adam and Eve were too smart to just roll over and give up the good life the first time someone came along touting the wonderful properties of magical beans. In other words, I do not think they were very naïve.

I wonder if the serpent talked to anyone who happened to venture by, while his real target was Adam. Adam probably would not talk to him—strictly obeying God. But the serpent knew Adam was the prize. Why is that?

Apparently, there was a challenge in place: Could Satan corrupt Adam, causing him to disobey the one rule God gave him? *Do not touch or eat of the Tree of Knowledge!* Reminds us of Job, doesn't it?

If Adam failed, Satan would gain a few things. The ability to:

1. Speak to the human subconscious mind directly, influencing decisions and actions.

2. Affect a person's health—directly and/or indirectly.

3. Possess certain human bodies with demons.

4. Work to ensure all children of Adam chose his rebellious ways instead of God's, who by default, would tend to lean in Satan's direction—the ways of the world.

5. And the consolation prize: Take possession of the Keys to Death and Hades (Rev 1:18)—the ability to capture and hold souls in his realm after people died.

Satan had a simple plan: Get to Adam through Eve.

He was patient in the patience of being immortal and able to out-wait just about any earthly situation. He talks to Eve. He works on her thinking and her mind, creating doubts and suspicions.

He tells Eve that God has held something back that would make her superior, wiser, and smarter. Like an infection that will not heal, the idea festers in her mind for ages until Eve decides to test it by doing something radical and expressly forbidden.

GENESIS 3

Serpent: *Did God really say, "You must not eat from any tree in the Garden?"* (Genesis 3:1, a half-truth—he knows exactly what God told them).

Adam: Present but apparently not the target of the question.

Eve corrects Serpent: *We may eat fruit from all of the trees in the Garden. But God did say, "You must not touch or eat the fruit from the tree that is in the middle of the Garden, or you will surely die."*

Serpent: *You will not surely die* (a lie). *For God knows that when you eat of it, your eyes will be opened, and you will be like God, knowing good and evil* (a truth, Gen 3:2-3).

There are two implications to his reply: First, apparently Serpent has slowly earned Eve's respect in matters related to God. He completely turns over what God said, boldly declaring it as a lie, and Eve does not run away screaming for help. Instead, she listens—intently. This implies that Serpent and Eve have not only talked before, but Serpent had challenged something else in relation to God, and in Eve's mind, Serpent was proven right. Moreover, why does it seem like only Eve and Serpent are involved in this conversation? Why didn't Adam jump up in alarm and drag her away?

Second, another implication of Serpent's comment is that God has not been fully honest and transparent with them. This must not be the first occasion where Serpent has pointed this out. Adam and Eve might not even understand what good and evil are, or how their knowing this information would bring benefit or harm. Nevertheless, Serpent has effectively sown distrust and doubt in God, probably many times before this final, fateful discourse. By suggesting that God has lied to them, by suggesting that he, Serpent, has more complete, or better, or exceptional information, the command by God to obey the one rule is circumvented, or at least minimized and disparaged.

"Half a truth is often a great lie," wrote Benjamin Franklin, and Satan is the resident expert of lies, half lies, and half truths.

I was watching a report about how deceitful people slowly gain the trust of seniors and then work to separate them from their life savings; and they are successful every single day, despite repeated warnings in magazines and on television. During tax season, people disguised as Internal Revenue Service (IRS) agents, goad people into sending them money. We are always amazed at how successful these thieves are. Why would someone share personal information over the phone with a person in a foreign country?

"Don't you want to be like God, darling?" Serpent asked.

From that time forward—from the Fall—we all act like little gods. Yes, we now know the difference between good and evil, but that does not mean we can effectively choose between the two and act accordingly. No. Instead, we weigh our choices by our desires, or our perceived personal needs. "Me! Me! Me!" has been the trumpet call since the Fall. We shout, "My needs, my wants, my interests are most important, especially more relevant than yours!" We often believe love works best when it serves our special needs. When it does not, then divorce has become the logical alternative in a post-Garden, fallen world.

Little gods. We must have control, driven like slaves before the master's whip. I must have control. I was enlisted—Air Force and Army—for ten years, and one reason I became an officer was to be in control, not always mindlessly saluting, taking orders, and doing someone else's bidding. I wanted to know what was going on and to then have the ability to shape what happened next. And I did. And I loved it, thriving in that environment.

Spend time watching children play and their arguments revolve around who controls what. Many arguments people have, especially couples, are about control. (No, I will not give you examples from my forty-plus-year marriage.) Russia wants to control Ukraine and steals Crimea, China creates islands to control the South China Sea, Iran wants to control its own destiny without outside influence, Palestine does not want Israel to control all of Jerusalem, and the examples go on and on, starting in individual lives, families, churches, institutions, businesses, and finally countries. Control starts with "I want . . ." and goes down from there—and has for thousands of years.

God wanted Adam to establish dominion over the world, and after a fashion, he and his children did. In harmony. Adam and his descendents were happy to live in cooperative tranquility with nature, essentially as gatherers and caretakers.

Because of its simplicity and wonder, I have heard people say they wished they could live on Pandora, the *Avatar* movie-created world, where unobtainium (an anti-gravity, superconducting mineral) is mined by human invaders. Our world, Earth, was once like Pandora. We have found that the descendents of Adam, before the Fall, made simple things: pots and bells, who knows what else. But they seemed to lack the drive for accomplishment that makes humans like us build the world we live in today—violent and terrifying as it often is. We do not see evidence in the rock and soil of cultures built like ours: concrete jungles, paved highways, steel superstructures, perhaps only the pyramids. The difference between the ancient, pre-Fall culture of Adam and us was part of Adam's curse. Instead of establishing dominion—governing authority, supervising creation, leaving a soft footprint on the earth (Gen 1:26), we divide and conquer, firmly planting our foot on Earth's neck, and each other.

Much of what Jesus came to tell us was that our ultimate, personal pleasure would only come when we gave control of our lives back to God. *"Consider the lilies of the field . . ."* (Matt 6:28; Luke 12:27). Jesus tried to explain that there is another source of pleasure our free will can choose—the knowledge and experience of God. The whole idea of the Kingdom of God was to implement, on purpose, the kind of living that once graced the Garden in the past and would be common on New Earth in the future.

Back to the conversation.

Adam. Silent. Watching. Waiting.

I find it curious that he seems somewhat disengaged from all of this. Had he heard this type of conversation many times before, so it put him to sleep? Did Eve drag him there against his will? Did he want Eve to fail, so he remains silent, somewhat passive aggressive? Why would that idea be true? Bottom line: Adam does not intervene.

Eve. Finally gives in.

What happened to push her over the edge into disobedience?

Besides Satan's promises of wisdom and knowledge, we read that Eve *"saw that the fruit of the tree was good for food and pleasing to the eye"* (Gen 3:6). Maybe that is why some people think the fruit was an apple, red in color with delicious stripes of yellow and gold; the air probably smelled pretty good sitting under that tree in season. The fruit would assail the senses on multiple levels—appearance, fragrance, taste. What kind of fruit it was did not matter. It could have been a banana or kiwi, but few people outside of New Zealand would say the kiwi was pleasing to the eye! Eating any type of off-limits fruit would garner the same result—and punishment.

Eve tentatively touches the forbidden fruit—does not die! Plucks the forbidden fruit—does not die! Eats—does not die!—amazed that she did not fall over dead. She looks around and offers some to cautious Adam, who is staring wild-eyed, wondering what all of this means. Is Serpent right and God wrong after all this time?

Adam touches and bites, juice running down his chin. It is the best thing he has ever tasted, and he does not fall over dead! Perhaps Serpent was right after all. He got this part right, didn't he? Why is Serpent laughing? Oh yeah, and what is death?

I have often wondered about another curse on Eve:

Your desire will be for your husband, and he will rule over you (Gen 3:16).

Why is that a curse? I know feminists who bristle at this idea. No man has ever "ruled" over them—never will. But what is happening here with Eve?

The first part of the curse is to create desire, so we can assume desire was probably not at the top of her everyday list. It could be that over a long time, it had waned, but there is a sense here that if God emphasizes it, then desire must have been lacking overall, from the beginning. Before the Fall, maybe sex had no drive or power to it, sort of a take it or leave it affair.

But the linking of *desire* with *rule* leads me to an overall level of subjection. It is easy to assume that desire is simply or mostly sexually related, but I think that minimizes the curse. Instead, I believe it was a more holistic expression: sex, emotions, mental perspective, physical attention. But think about this: The curse would be more poignant if she had ruled over him and his desire was out of place in the relationship. A course correction would be necessary.

He will rule over you.

I believe that in the Garden, over a great length of time, a matriarchal society developed with Eve making all decisions, especially the important ones. The curse would reverse this trend, placing Adam, and men, again as the leaders and rulers.

How did the Garden become a matriarchal society?

Nature abhors a vacuum.

With the increase in children and population, people might think a little guidance and rules were required for things like playing, sharing, mating, living areas and shelter, food gathering, water source protection, behavior, disagreements, and waste disposal. "Hey you; poop somewhere else—not over there where the kids are playing!"

Over time, the Garden was probably feeling a little smaller, crowded. Someone would need to take charge, willing to step up by leading, directing, making decisions, and helping people with choices. Someone needed to lead.

So where was Adam?

Let us consider two possibilities.

God gave Adam a mandate—name the animals, rule over all creation—fill it, subdue it (Gen 1-2). I know this injunction probably meant more than just giving them names: that in the naming, he would come to understand the creatures and grow into something like a shepherd, watching, guiding, and caring. Especially if some of the animals were already prone to being livestock (Gen 1:26). I can imagine sheep supplying milk and cheese. They've been domesticated so long they probably cannot survive without shepherds.

I have wondered if, over a very long time, Adam named the animals in the Garden and then wandered, exploring outside—accompanied by a few children, studying and naming all creatures, great and small, wherever he found them (Gen 1:28). The Garden might have been located in or on the border of what we now know as Africa—conveniently centered on one great continent.

The land mass of Earth was quite different back then: one large super continent called Pangea. The Bible mentions rivers surrounding the Garden. I can imagine deep river canyons around the Garden, isolating it from other parts of the earth, thereby keeping out the larger voracious carnivores. At first, Adam could explore and find his way home without the need to sail a boat across great oceans: they didn't separate land masses yet. Even the tallest mountain range would have been relatively flat by modern standards, since mountain ranges formed later when the continental tectonic plates broke apart and collided.

We know from archeological evidence that all manner of creatures covered the planet, but the planet was one large landmass, easily accessible to Adam and his kids. Exploring. Immortal. In communion with God. And gone from the Garden for extended periods.

Another idea occurred to me, less romantic than the first. I wonder if Adam was not highly motivated—laid back. Naming animals, exploring, skipping rocks on the river, mating once in a while, hanging out with God, following bees to a hive dripping with honey, picking bananas and berries along the river, learning to swim, playing ball with Dog, enjoying life, helping with the kids if it suited him, taking naps in the warm afternoon sun by the pond. Life was easy and the livin' was good—extraordinarily good. Physically present, but not available or caring to make decisions.

If the first-created, Adam, was not present or willing to step up and take charge by leading, directing, making decisions, and helping people with choices, then who would? The second-created—Eve—the mother of us all, would feel obligated, even forced begrudgingly, to occupy the space not assumed by Adam. I am guessing Adam was quite happy to let it happen; he had more important things to do, whether exploring the world, supervising creation, or living in abject contentment.

Of course, Serpent was involved every step of the way; perhaps just by suggesting that Eve take charge when needs arose, adding a dash of flattery and then praising her for any accomplishments, big and small. He would become a positive and encouraging influence, an affirmative voice in her life, especially if Adam did not particularly care one way or the other, or was seldom around. If out exploring, he could be gone an incredibly long time, and Eve would learn to trust Serpent, who always managed to be close by when needed.

Adam never had to work a day in his long life, so God's curse for him is what? Make that boy a farmer! *"Through painful toil"* (Gen 3:17).

To make matters worse, the ground would resist him every step of the way.

It (the ground) *will produce thorns and thistles for you, and you will eat the plants of the field* (Gen 3:18).

I think the idea here is that in the Garden, they could just pluck and eat whatever was at hand—a tremendous variety of fruits, nuts, and vegetables. They may have even harvested wild wheat to make simple bread. Now food would be difficult to come by, elusive and seasonal. They would have to sow seeds, cultivate and harvest crops to provide food in winter and during the lean times, and for seeds the following year.

The earliest known domesticated crops were: cereals—wheat, barley, rye, oats, millet; pulses—lentils, peas, chickpeas, beans; oils and fibers—flax, hemp, cotton; fruit and nuts—olives, grapes, figs, dates, pomegranates, apples, pears, plums, cherries, carobs, almonds, walnuts, chestnuts, hazels, pistachios; vegetables and tubers—melons, leeks, garlic, onions, lettuce, cabbage, turnips, beets, carrots, celery.[1]

Lots of possible food options, and I am guessing God helped them get things going with suggestions and maybe even demonstrations, since he seems to be almost as present outside the Garden as inside (ref. Cain's comment to God on his punishment, Gen 4:13–14, *"Today you are driving me from the land, and I will be hidden from your presence"*).

As it suited them, some people would become farmers and others herders in order to survive (Gen 4:2, *Now Abel kept flocks, and Cain worked the soil*). Genesis 1:26 tells us that God made some animals prone to domestication, and we know sheep and goats were domesticated early on. Soon after the Fall, Abel already had animals for the annual sacrifice.

Now the basic needs of food, clothing, and shelter would drive the human race and societies, along with an exponential increase in pride, feeding a growing quest for the best land, resources, power, control, and advantages over others. Competition for these essentials would bring most people into conflict, and life would be a struggle with no guarantees—and little hope.

Adam's new jobs would be planting and weeding, if they were to survive outside the Garden.

By the sweat of your brow you will eat your food until you return to the ground, since from it you were taken; for dust you are and to dust you will return (Gen 3:19)—a lonely mantra I have recited at many funerals.

Hey Adam! The extended season of contentment has finally come to an end. Life will be hard for the first time in your exceedingly long life, and your immortal days are over. Have a nice day! So farming is actually the oldest profession—not something else. Enter the dawn of agriculture and the joys of weeding.

I came across an article relevant to our discussion here.

The agricultural revolution was one of the most profound events in human history, leading to the rise of modern civilization. Now, in the first study of its kind, an international team of scientists has found that after agriculture arrived in Europe 8,500 years ago, people's DNA underwent widespread changes, altering their height, digestion, immune system and skin color.[2]

Isn't it interesting that biblical scholars, based on the study of Adam's genealogy, believe Adam and Eve were ejected from the Garden about 8,500 years ago?

Early Europeans lived as hunter-gatherers for over 35,000 years. About 8,500 years ago, farmers left their first mark in the archaeological record of the continent.[3]

The concluding paragraph sums it up well:

Before the rise of agriculture, Europe was home to a population of hunter-gatherers. Then a wave of people arrived whose DNA resembles that of people in the Near East. It's likely that they brought agriculture with them.[4]

People from the Near East; fits well with all I have been saying here, doesn't it?

God had Adam and Eve driven out of the Garden. Could it get any worse? Definitely yes. Because the curse on Adam and Eve from the Fall would be passed down through the generations to every child born *outside the Garden*, for all time. Adam and Eve could not go back into the Garden and neither could their unfortunate family. Their children's children would be farmers and herders, at odds with nature and each other, with no sign of relief in sight.

In a few generations, Lamech bragged:

"I have killed a man for wounding me, a young man for injuring me. If Cain is avenged seven times, then Lamech seventy-seven times" (Gen 4:23-24; Matt 18:21-22).

A sense of lawlessness quickly permeates this new society, and the pride of revenge drives Lamech's haughty life. A short time later, God would lament, "... *every inclination of the thoughts of man's heart was only evil all the time*" (Gen 6:5). Do you hear the note of despair?

Now the war in heaven had finally spilled over into our world with the fate of the human race at stake.

Before we leave this section, I want to point out that Adam and the early descendants probably lived long lives outside the Garden, post-Fall, as a side effect of being perfect human specimens. The perfect genome degenerated with each generation. The lifespan slowly dropped, because the descendants of Adam could not eat from the Tree of Life. Only nineteen generations later, Abraham lives to 175 years, his son Isaac to 180, and by the time we get to King David—fourteen generations from Abraham, he dies at 70 years old, which became our new standard.

BIBLICAL

CHAPTER NINE

ALIENS

We have established that there is a war, which has gone on for ages and ages, and will reach its climax just before the great ship arrives. So who is fighting and why? Let us look at some of the players in this conflict.

The Bible describes a multi-aspect being, angels of all kinds, dragons, soul catchers, and by inference, the Ancient Ones, which you will find interesting, because it includes space aliens. And they are all here—now. What a wonderful array of aliens living and fighting on our front porch. Just rich. Who needs books on fantasy and science fiction when we have the Bible?

MULTI-ASPECT BEING

If you were watching a science fiction movie and a creature entered made up of three distinct other creatures, yet with shared *and separate* minds, you would just take it all in stride, not needing to understand the personal or psychological implications or complications of such a being. You would think, *Let's see what happens, how it interacts in the story with the plot and characters.*

Through popular movies like *Indian Jones and the Crystal Skull* (2008), H. G. Wells' *The First Men in the Moon* (1901), the Borg cybernetic organisms of the *Star Trek* series (1996), other movies, and a host of novels, most of us have all heard of the hive mind. In fact, it might be that certain ants, termites, bees, and aspen trees operate on some such level as directed by pheromones, airborne chemicals, electric pulses—voltage-based signaling, or something we do not fully understand.

And yet, that is how God has revealed himself to us, what theologians call the Trinity. Some people struggle with this idea, saying, "It doesn't make sense." I agree. But isn't it like a bacteria trying to understand humans? Incomprehensible. You just have to say, *Interesting . . . we'll just see what happens in the story with the plot and characters.*

Let's entertain some what if's.

To communicate better with us, a wise alien would not land a spaceship on the White House lawn, making the Secret Service grumpy. If the being had the capability, especially if he had created us and our world, he might instead choose to be born among us to experience what it was like to be fully human. He would become a person we could actually relate to and hopefully understand.

And how would this *God-among-us* act? In first-century Israel, an aspiring rabbi had to be 30 years old to speak authoritatively on any subject. He might talk about life in the other realm where he came from, teaching us how to live a full life, while inviting us to join him—under certain conditions, of course.

What if that alien who created us also chose to communicate through the living systems around us and what we would call nature. What if the alien human came to teach the bacteria how to ascend to the human form, telling us that something was built into the bacteria profile by the same creature that would allow us to be transformed upon death into a human.

Bah humbug!—some will cry.

Isn't that what happens when a caterpillar transforms into a butterfly? Metamorphosis—a completely new creature—from crawling in the dirt to flying. Radical. It seems to me that nature has left us clues on a small scale about what happens on a larger scale. The Apostle Paul wrote:

For since the creation of the world God's invisible qualities—his eternal power and divine nature—have been clearly seen, being understood from what has been made, so that people are without excuse (Romans 1:20).

This is probably why so many people feel something special—a spiritual connection—when out in primitive, unspoiled nature. Rainbows and colorful sunrises cause us to stop with appreciation. We marvel at the television programs about animal behavior and mysteries of the earth.

But ask the animals, and they will teach you, or the birds in the sky, and they will tell you; or speak to the earth, and it will teach you, or let the fish in the sea inform you. Which of all these does not know that the hand of the LORD has done this? In his hand is the life of every creature and the breath of all mankind" (Job 12:7-10).

And if we do not understand this passage in our head, our heart likely does.

At the beginning of the Bible we read, *"In the beginning God created the heavens and the earth"* (Gen 1:1). Don't you find it interesting that the word for God here is *Elohim*— and plural? Also, the *im* ending indicates a plural masculine noun. In English, it sounds like a singular word—*God*—an individual. God did this. God did that. But this is how it really reads:

So Gods [Elohim] *created humans in their own image, in the image of Gods* [Elohim] *they created them; male and female they created them* (Gen 1:27).

Here are two verses in Matthew, where we see all three:

As soon as Jesus was baptized, he went up out of the water. At that moment heaven was opened, and he saw the Spirit of God descending like a dove and alighting on him. And a voice from heaven said, "This is my Son, whom I love; with him I am well pleased" (Matt 3:16-17).

Not only do we have the biblical concept of God the Father, God the Son, and God the Holy Spirit (John 10:30), but there is an intrinsic maleness and femaleness built into the fabric of their unity and being. We read that they created us *in their image—male and female*. Males and females are different physically and psychologically, but the sum of us—together—equals what would essentially be the nature and being of God(s). Two related to one. Is it any wonder that God hates divorce? (Malachi 2:16).

Another aspect of this relationship, and mark of our Creator, is our own triune nature: body, soul, and spirit. The body is easy enough to understand, but confusion begins when resolving the difference between soul and spirit.

I have heard the soul described as our emotional and mental self, while the spirit gives life. However, I believe the "self," that part that makes each of us unique, is intertwined in both our soul and spirit.

Jesus and the Apostle Paul both described dead people as being asleep (Mark 5:39; John 11:11; 1 Thessalonians 4:13). Paul said, *"We are confident moreover, and are pleased, to be absent out of the body and to be* at home *with the Lord"* (2 Cor 5:8, literal Greek: "at home" can mean "present"), meaning that at death a person is present with God. Jesus told the believing thief on the cross next to him that that day they would be together in Paradise (Luke 23:43)—sounds like they will be alive somewhere, not dead and unconscious and cold in a tomb or buried in the ground. I know people who believe that way—lights out at death, nothing follows.

At death, the body begins to decompose. In the ocean, it dissolves completely and disappears. But another part of us—the soul, is asleep. Our spirit departs this place, going to the spiritual dimension, still very much alive and aware. We are fully in both places as ourselves: the soul sleeping near where the body died or is buried, and the spirit in heaven actively engaged with whatever is going on there.

Confusing? Sounds a lot like our problem with God and the Trinity, doesn't it?

There is a preponderance of circumstantial evidence for life after death, of people dying and being in the presence of friends, angels, and God. As a hospice chaplain, I regularly met with patients, who nearing their departure—within a week or two, sometimes longer—described seeing angels and previously departed loved ones. I learned that nearly every person who dies gets an escort by an angel or relative, which I believe is to comfort the dying person and the family; it certainly comforted me. And to give us hope.

Being in the presence of people who are seeing and having conversations with angels and the previously departed builds your faith and creates a deep-seated hope and expectation of *life* after death. Life goes on, uninterrupted, so the act of dying is simply a momentary, yet uninterrupted, transition period. The body dies, the spirit ascends to heaven (since the time of Jesus), and there is a sense that the soul is sleeping, awaiting the resurrection in a new body.

I do not know why it was set up this way. God thought it was important. I have wondered if that is a difference between us and angels, that angels are not triune. God made us in his image, and God is plural, a triune being. But I know that the reunion of soul and spirit—in a new body, based on the old one, at the resurrection, is of paramount importance. Why? It seems that we are incomplete—partial and less—until that happens: A transformed butterfly without wings.

The Apostle Paul, talking about the resurrected Christ, wrote:

His purpose was to create in himself one new man out of two (Eph 2:15).

Is that the answer?—that even now, we are three parts but not a whole with the body dominant? We glimpse those other parts, imperfectly, when our spirits soar with rapturous feelings, or we feel the profound presence of the Holy Spirit. In our new body, we will become one—undivided: body-soul-spirit perfectly united, perfectly equal, a new creature—in the image of God.

The resurrection is a specific moment in time: the reuniting of body, soul, and spirit. At the return of Jesus to Earth in the Second Coming, we learn that a final trumpet will sound. At that time, a resurrection event takes place.

> For the Lord himself will come down from heaven, with a loud command, with the voice of the archangel and with the trumpet call of God, and the dead in Christ will rise first . . . (1 Thess 4:16).

Why does the resurrection happen? I believe this resurrection happens at that specific time—at the sound of *the last trumpet*, to reward us with the opportunity to witness the Second Coming. Perhaps we will also join the armies of heaven in some capacity in the final conquest.

There is a sense that if you want to believe certain things you have to take other matters on faith. I am guessing that all of our questions will be answered—eventually, but perhaps not in this lifetime. We are like kids asking *why* all the time. I try to explain the why's to my grandson. But while he knows enough to ask the questions, at his tender young age he does not have the ability to understand many of the answers. In time, when he is older, he will grasp the explanations, the new ideas, and figure out some things on his own so he can help others. And so it goes.

By being Trinitarian creatures ourselves, we are a step closer to comprehending God—by intention, and according to that scripture, probably equipped intuitively to understand many things. I have heard people explain that when they came to know God—personally (which is my testimony as well), the experience seemed to complete them, filling a spiritual void inside—a sense of emptiness, restlessness, and search for meaning—which only God could fill. Years spent trying to fill the void with other things—even religion, leaves us empty until we find that perfect fit—God.

ANGELS

The term *angel* seems to be an all-encompassing category for some of the sentient creatures God created in the spiritual universe. It might be that all types of creatures in the spiritual realm are angels, although they have different shapes and functions and represent different races. The Bible mentions angels throughout, and people have written many books on the subject. Mostly they are described as creatures similar to us, although some apparently have wings (Zech 5:9, *"They had wings like those of a stork . . ."*), a few are strangely put together, and many walk around armed—the archangel Michael. When they appear on Earth, many look and act just like you and me.

Do not forget to show hospitality to strangers, for by so doing some people have shown hospitality to angels without knowing it (Heb 13:2).

That statement was true when Hebrews was written and true today: Aliens among us—today.

In Genesis 18, three visitors appear to Abraham, who insists they stay for dinner. Two of these men go on to Sodom to rescue Abraham's nephew, Lot, and his family. Abraham and Lot both immediately recognized these men for what they were—angels—just by looking at them. Was it their clothes, their bearing, previous visits, beardless faces, unlined perfect skin, the Ray-Ban sunglasses?

We know angels are messengers. Gabriel went to the prophet Daniel with a message (Dan 9:21), and later another angel explains to Daniel that he would have returned sooner with an answer to his prayer, *"but the prince of the Persian kingdom resisted me twenty-one days. Then Michael, one of the chief princes, came to help me"* (Dan 10:13). This passage describes some kind of conflict in the heavenly realms. When praying to God, do angels carry our prayers to him and bring back the response? Is that their primary role as messengers?

And another angel came and stood at the altar, having a golden censer; and there was given unto him much incense, that he should offer it with the prayers of all the saints—and the smoke of the incense, which came with the prayers of the saints, ascended up before God out of the angel's hand (Rev 8:3–4; and Jacob's Ladder of Gen 28:12; Rev 5:8).

We can learn something from King David. From experience, he understood prayer in his relationship with God:

O LORD, I call to you; come quickly to me. Hear my voice when I call to you. May my prayer be set before you like incense; may the lifting of my hands be like the evening sacrifice (Psalm 141:1-2).

David talks to God. He has an expectation of a quick response and God's personal intervention in answer to his request. It really does not matter if angels carry his prayers—or ours.

Let me pause here a second.

Do angels carry all of our prayers? Some passages suggest that angels carry certain prayers, but Jesus told the disciples (and us):

And I will do whatever you ask in my name, so that the Son may bring glory to the Father. You may ask me for anything in my name and I will do it (John 14:13-14).

This goes along with the admonition in the book of Hebrews: *"Let us then approach the throne of grace* (God's throne) *with confidence, so that we may receive mercy and find grace to help us in our time of need"* (Heb 4:16).

SUMMARY

We pray to God in the name of Jesus. The Bible promises that we have direct access to God without the intervention of angels or saints. At the same time, angels may also collect or carry our prayers for other purposes.

Luke chapter 1 describes the angel Gabriel visiting Mary, telling her she would have a child called the Son of the Most High. And you all know the Christmas story: how a great company of the heavenly hosts appeared to the shepherds praising God and saying:

Glory to God in the highest, and on earth peace, good will toward all people (Luke 2:13-14).

However, the part we are interested in is from Revelation 12:7-9:

And there was war in heaven. Michael and his angels fought against the dragon, and the dragon and his angels fought back. But he [the dragon] *was not strong enough, and they lost their place in heaven.*

Evidence in the Bible—Old and New Testaments—and from current affairs, tells us the battle has not yet ended. The battle will rage until the return of Jesus, and even that period of peace is temporary.

Two angels appear to be leaders: The Bible specifically mentions Gabriel and Michael (Michael in Jude 1:9; Rev 12:7; Dan 10:13, 21, Dan 12:1; Gabriel in Dan 8:16, 9:21; Luke 1:19, 26). The Bible presents Michael as an archangel and always fighting, while Gabriel always delivers messages.

Note: The word *lucifer* is not a name at all, much less for Satan, but rather a mistranslation of Isaiah 14:12, which should read, *"How you have fallen from heaven, bright one, son of the dawn."* Isaiah is describing the fall of Satan, but *lucifer* simply means "bright one" and is not a proper noun. Satan can appear as an angel of light, as it suits him, so "bright one" is appropriate—at times (2 Cor 11:14). And lucifer absolutely does not mean Morning Star, as some translations have grossly mistranslated the word (NIV, New Living Translation, English Standard Version, New American Standard, King James, International Standard Version, and more). The only Bible versions to get it right are the NET Bible and Young's Literal Translation. Good work, folks.

Angels help people in times of need, although we may not realize it. *"Are not angels ministering spirits sent to serve those who will inherit salvation?"* (Heb 1:14). The angels helped Jesus after his forty-day fast (Matt 4:11).

I know people who see angels.

I had a hospice patient with face cancer; her whole right side was missing—eye, skin, muscle. Tough. She wore a veil over part of her face, but you still caught glimpses. On one visit, she told me that late at night, when it was calm and quiet in the skilled nursing facility, a man came and stood on the right side of her bed *and she could see him.* "How could that be?" she asked.

I explained to her that the visitor was an angel—a spiritual creature, and she saw him with her *spiritual* right eye, which was working just fine. The nightly "visions" continued and brought her great peace in her final days, and we were able to plumb the depths of her faith and hope. An angel ministered to her at a crucial time, and she died peacefully a week later. Hospice nurses, caregivers, and chaplains have many stories like this.

STRANGE CREATURES

God created many strange creatures for specific tasks—cherubim, seraphim, and others. Some non-biblical Jewish and Christian literature describe hierarchies of angels and powers. However, when these descriptions depart from the Bible, some seem rather imaginative, and there is no way to know if they are true or made up.

The Bible is full of the strange and fanciful.

In the center, around the throne, were four living creatures, and they were covered in eyes, in front and in back. The first living creature was like a LION, the second was like an OX, the third had a face like a MAN, and the fourth was like a flying EAGLE. Each of the four living creatures had six wings and was covered with eyes all around, even under his wings (Rev 4:6-8, also Ezek 1:10).

These creatures have one purpose:

Day and night they never stop saying: Holy, holy, holy is the LORD God Almighty, who was, and is, and is to come" (Rev 4:8).

Something we say every Sunday during Holy Communion in the Anglican Church.

Why do these creatures appear like this: a man, an ox, a lion, an eagle? I have wondered if they are a symbolic metaphor for reasons we cannot imagine (some have attributed them to the four Gospels), or if they represent something more. Do they personify four civilizations on other planets or spiritual dimensions, worshiping the Living God?

The human-like creature represents us, but what of the others? Is there a civilization of raptor-like people, another of great cats (which of course got me thinking of Aslan of the *Narnia* series), and another similar to bulls and cows—bovine, grass grazers? All intelligent, all capable of vibrant, thriving civilizations, where they worship and celebrate God. Could these other civilizations be struggling with satanic forces, like us, so that these four might represent God's ultimate victory in each civilization? Are they worshiping him, circling the throne, because they won (or will win) the chance to do just that?

God can make any creature on the earth intelligent, self-aware, capable of speech, with a vibrant culture, language, religion, art, and self-determination. In addition, every creature on Earth could be the premier species on their own planet, if God chose to make it happen. With so many planets in the universe (60 billion planets in the Milky Way alone), many variations of this idea are possible. Perhaps we will have a role in either participating in a Congress of the Created or in shepherding developing civilizations.

Earth is in the Outer Rim of the Orion Arm of the Milky Way, far from the galactic center. Would it surprise you to learn that other species have thrived on planets in our galaxy, developing great civilizations, and we were sort of late to the table?[1]

Imagine a Congress of the Created made up of nearly every possible creature we have on Earth, only incredibly and wonderfully intelligent. Because even a donkey can speak, if God chooses:

> Then the LORD opened the donkey's mouth, and it said to Balaam, "What have I done to you to make you beat me these three times?" (Numbers 22:28).

CHAPTER TEN

DRAGONS

CHERUBIM

God can create anything, and it seems he created a dragon—at least one, although there could be more, perhaps a host of dragons or dragon-like, reptilian beings. Maybe that is why a third of the angels fell with Satan; they were also dragons or of a similar angelic reptilian species. That would explain some of the modern stories surrounding alien reptilian-like encounters.

The book of Job, chapter 41, speaks of a Leviathan creature that could only be a dragon. Look at the specifics: can't be caught by fishing with hooks or harpoons, speaks, double coat of armor, a back with rows of scales, fire comes out of mouth, smoke from nostrils, loves the depths of the ocean, nothing on earth its equal. At this point, the description might be a talking, fire-breathing crocodile, or a scaly prehistoric sea creature. But then we read, *"It looks down on all that are haughty; it is the king over all that are proud"* (Job 41:34). King of the Proud.

The prophet Isaiah talks about a flying serpent.

> *Rejoice not thou, whole Palestina, because the rod of him that smote thee is broken:* *for out of the serpent's root shall come forth a cockatrice, and his fruit shall be a fiery* *flying serpent* (Isaiah 14:29 KJV; some translators have changed "flying serpent" to "darting adder," but this is actually an accurate translation of the Hebrew).

Isn't it interesting that every major culture references dragons? From a passage in Ezekiel 28, I believe that this dragon is a type of angel—a cherub. Cherubim are guardian angels who watch over something God has determined important. Some cherubim descriptions sound like humans with wings, while others sound like dragons.

Guardian Cherubs on top of Ark of Covenant.

The two angels on top of the Ark of the Covenant are cherubs.

Make one cherub at one end and one cherub at the other end; you shall make the cherubim of one piece with the mercy seat at its two ends. The cherubim shall have their wings spread upward, covering the mercy seat with their wings and facing one another; the faces of the cherubim are to be turned toward the mercy seat (Exodus 25:19-20).

However, these two-winged cherubs are quite different from the cherub called Satan. Whom do you think this passage is about?

This is what the Sovereign LORD says: "You were the seal of perfection, full of wisdom and perfect in beauty. You were in the Garden of Eden, the Garden of God; every precious stone adorned you . . . Your settings and mountings were made of gold . . .You were anointed as a Guardian Cherub . . . You were on the holy mount of God; you walked among the fiery stones. You were blameless in your ways from the day you were created till wickedness was found in you—So I drove you in disgrace from the mount of God, and I expelled you, Guardian Cherub, from among the fiery stones. Your heart became proud on account of your beauty, and you corrupted your wisdom because of your splendor. So I threw you to the earth; I made a spectacle of you before kings" (Ezek 28:12-17).

The description here sounds like a dragon with scales covered in gold and precious stones. Beautiful. Wonderful. An anointed guardian cherub of the cherubim angel race. Unaffected by fire, perhaps preferring it. Because of his beauty and intelligence, a great pride came upon him and violence, so God cast him down. There is no pride in God and no creature with pride can stand before him (James 4:6).

However, it was much more than pride at work in Satan. He wanted to rule, and he especially wanted others to worship him.

How art thou fallen from heaven, bright one, son of the morning! How art thou cut down to the ground, which didst weaken the nations! For thou hast said in thine heart, I will ascend into heaven, I will exalt my throne above the stars of God: I will sit also upon the mount of the congregation, in the sides of the north: I will ascend above the heights of the clouds; I will be like the Most High (Isaiah 14:12-14, KJV).

Sometimes Isaiah is the voice of God, speaking prophecy or telling a story. In the next passage, God is speaking of Babylon, but Satan is the real subject.

You have trusted in your wickedness and have said, "No one sees me." Your wisdom and knowledge mislead you when you say to yourself, "I AM, and there is none besides me." Disaster will come upon you. (Isaiah 47:10-11).

No, Isaiah is not talking about Babylon. One thing we learn from this verse is that Satan even called himself the great I AM, which is YHWH—pronounced "Yah-way," also pronounced "Jehovah" by some. Satan not only wanted to be greater than God, he wanted to actually be God. Is that even possible? What deranged, maniacal mind could comprehend and desire that?

When Moses asked God what his name was, he replied:

I AM WHO I AM. This is what you are to tell the Israelites: "I AM has sent me to you" (Exodus 3:14).

I find it incredible that a created being would aspire to replace God and be God, ruling all creation in his place, or trying to.

Only one other person claimed to be the I AM, and when he did, the Pharisees picked up rocks to stone him: Jesus—*and he was God.* (John 4:26, 6:20, 8:24, 38, 58; 13:19, 18:5–6). The prophet Isaiah said, *"The virgin will be with child and will give birth to a son, and will call him Emmanuel,"* which means *God With Us* (Isaiah 7:14, also Matt 1:23). Because Jesus is part of the Trinity, he could tell people he was indeed *God With Us*—in the flesh. Messiah means "Anointed One." The name Christ is the Greek translation of "Messiah." Jesus Christ in the Greek is the same as Joshua Messiah in the Hebrew. Yes, the disciples could have called him Josh—perhaps at times, at first.

Mormons believe God created all spirits, including Jesus and Satan. Although they do not expressly say Jesus and Satan are brothers, they believe Jesus and Satan are created beings, so, "We are all brothers and sisters to Christ, and so well as to Satan." In an attempt at clarification, they write, "Mormons believe God created all things. We are his children. Jesus and Satan were both sons of God in the beginning, and thus it is technically correct that Mormons believe Jesus and Satan once were brothers—in this sense."[2] Same result, because Christians believe Jesus was never created; he is fully God. To suggest otherwise would negate the incarnation, so that Jesus could not authoritatively tell the Pharisees he was the I AM, would not be Emmanuel, and, therefore, unqualified to die on the cross for all sins. Once again, suggesting that Jesus and Satan are equal or were equal, in any sense, would make Satan equal with God, one of his obvious and stated goals. Joseph Smith received these revelations from angels.

So for Satan to state that he was God would mean he wanted to put God into a place where he would not interfere—not killed (if that is even possible) but locked up or controlled somehow, which would include all leaders and the armies following God in the heavenly realms. If Satan can imagine such an outcome and even states his intention by calling himself God, does that mean it is actually possible, somehow, however remote? Or is this just the delusional ranting of a psychopathic madman? Mad angel?

There are passages in the Bible, like this one we just read from Isaiah 47:10–11, that make me think Satan does not buy into the idea that God is omniscient—knowing all things, seeing ahead of time what will happen. Does Satan think that at any time in the past, he has outsmarted God? Surprised God? Blindsided him? Makes a person wonder.

Let me pause here a second, because this idea of God being surprised is in the Bible, and some of you reading this will wonder if the passage applies:

The people of Judah have done evil in my eyes, declares the LORD. They have set up their detestable idols in the house that bears my NAME and have defiled it. They have built the high places of Topheth in the Valley of Ben Hinnom to burn their sons and daughters in the fire—something I did not command nor did it enter my mind (Jer 7:30-31).

You know I have scratched my head over this one a few times. This statement appears two more times in Jeremiah 19:5 and 32:35, and nowhere else, so you begin to think God really did not know. How can we reconcile his surprise with a God who says he is the Alpha and Omega, knowing the end from the beginning—knowing all real and potential actions (Isaiah 46:10)?

The Hebrew translation of Jeremiah 7:31 says, "*It did not enter my heart.*" The Hebrew word *labe* means "heart," not mind. In the third century BC, scholars translated the Hebrew Bible into Greek, and they also used the word *cardia* or heart.

Why would anyone want to translate either word as mind?

These translations use mind instead of heart: New International Version, King James Version, New King James Version, Revised Standard Version. But the New American Standard has heart written in the margin. Does this really make a difference?

Poor scholarship is at work here, and the translation does make a difference. These verses in Jeremiah would then read, "*. . . nor did it enter my heart.*" This would mean that God knew the event would happen—with his omniscient mind, but their immoral and wicked behavior still broke his heart. Knowing you are right about the wreck of human choices does not make it easier to swallow. How many parents have watched their children make poor choices, and despaired? (Also Ezek 5:7-10.)

The Bible mentions Satan by name in some places and infers in others. Satan is not the opposite of God. He would like you to believe that, because it would make him roughly equal with God. In his great hubris, this "angelic" creature decided he could run things better than God could. The idea of being "like the Most High" or calling himself the I AM, means he wanted to be worshiped: above all, better than everyone.

Nevertheless, Satan, like us, is a created being. As the Creator of all things, only God is worthy of worship, honor, and glory.

PRIDE

C. S. Lewis said pride was the sin we are least aware of in ourselves because it carries a spiritual component directly from the depths of hell.[1]

Satan is the father of pride. Not the pride of a parent for a child's accomplishments, but the pride that thinks it is better than someone else—for whatever reason. The pride that says, my needs trump your needs, or I always know better than you what is needed or required in this or that situation. I deserve this. I am the king of my fate, the captain of my destiny and life. Look what I have done—ain't I special? There's no one like me.

This willful pride is the sign of a damaged heart and mind; and to make matters worse, we children of Adam come by it naturally. I think the entrance of pride into our DNA is the real curse that came from the failure of Adam and Eve in the Garden. For many of us, it is our bread and butter, as much a part of us as eating and breathing. For someone to suggest that there is a problem in this area of our lives is to invite unbridled wrath and indignation.

Unheard of! You want to correct me? How dare you! You, you, you little—

With God's help, I am always dealing with my pride, which makes me hypersensitive to it in others. Like a smoker who quits, then not able to tolerate being around other smokers.

Let me explain: I was reading *Mere Christianity* and thought I would skip the chapter on the Great Sin as a waste of time. Pride? I did not have pride. But for continuity's sake, I read anyhow: I couldn't say I read the book if I skipped a chapter, right? At the end, Lewis wrote, "If you think you are not conceited, it means you are very conceited indeed." I was shocked. It occurred to me that I did not really know what conceit (pride) was. I closed the book and prayed to God to show me, teach me. Over the next two weeks, whenever I said or did something prideful, a voice spoke in my head, saying, *"And that is pride!"* A painful and revealing school (1 Cor 2:13; 1 John 2:27).

The idea of the Holy Spirit taking someone to school, teaching directly, is not new. Rather, it is a promise.

> But the Counselor, the Holy Spirit, whom the Father will send in my name, he will teach you all things, and bring to your remembrance all that I have said to you (John 14:26).

Although God privileged me with this instruction, I must report (or confess) that I still struggle with pride and probably always will. But I sure know when it raises its ugly head, especially in others.

Side note on pride and the critical spirit.

A critical spirit is vocal pride, bullying from a distance, or bullying designed to assault directly or indirectly. I liken a critical spirit in someone to an open wound that will not heal—putrid, smelling, and gangrenous. The person is sick and does not know it, or does not care.

Have you ever met someone who was always complaining? I know people who complain, moan, criticize, and run people down, appraising others against themselves, expressing constant disapproval while spreading the blame. These sarcastic and cynical barbs are often disguised as a simple opinion or dark humor but are actually thinly veiled hostility, resentment, and scorn—even leveled against themselves at times. I have seen the critical spirit used to bully people brutally. Negative criticism is the opposite of praise, honor, and love, and nourishes a person's pride.

There are lots of problems and corruptions in the world. Some people and institutions (and even a few churches) define themselves by what they are against. As a pastor, I wanted to ensure that people in our church did not break up into groups arguing about what they were for and against, like watching for smoke and putting it out before a fire started. Some people were grumpy about what was going on in another church; another was grumpy about a particular form of worship. In certain years, politics were problematic. Smoke trails. What coffee should we use on Sunday mornings—Folgers or Starbucks? I noticed that certain people had a knack for stirring things up, whatever group they ended up in. Nothing was good enough for them—ever.

When I say, *let something go,* I do not mean you should not fight against injustice or wickedness or wrongdoing. Rather, focus on what you are "for," take the positive high ground. Do not let the negative force be the thing that drives you at the expense of growing in your faith and relationship with God.

For healing to take place, the Spirit of Criticism needs to be recognized in a life and then purposefully and consistently addressed—with the Holy Spirit's help and with the help of friends and loved ones. It must go away for a person to grow in their faith as a disciple and human being. It might require prayerful intervention, where loved ones confront the offender—in love, expressing their concerns.

Remember, either this is a habit of life the person learned on their own or from others, or an old and deep wound, which caused the critical spirit to manifest itself, originally, probably as a defense mechanism. At first, do not expect much; the critical person will feel attacked. They will deflect your concern, leveling the criticism at you with practiced and deft precision. They will turn your concern on its head, and you will be the one accused, criticized for your misguided efforts. Be in constant prayer, seeking God's help in opening their eyes, and keep trying. If all else fails, just keep asking God's Holy Spirit to bring healing and restoration in that life. That's how it worked for me.

And if you reading this are the critical person, ask God—every day—to transform you from the inside out. More on this idea later.

Skillfully using pride as a weapon, Satan told Adam and Eve they could be like God. Interestingly, this is Satan's own failing. A dangerous creature. He is not only the father of pride; he knows it and does not care.

And this rebellion has been going on for a long time.

At the creation of earth, all of the angels—the sons of God—rejoiced, Satan among them.

> *Where were you when I laid the foundation of the earth? Tell me, if you have understanding . . . When the morning stars sang together, and all the sons of God shouted for joy?* (Job 38:4, 7 KJV).

This scripture gives us an idea of the timing, when things happened, and where everyone stood. At the creation of our universe, the angels rejoiced. I believe Satan saw creation as a personal opportunity, which is exactly what God wanted him to see.

> *And another sign appeared in heaven: and behold, a great red dragon having seven heads and ten horns, and on his heads were seven diadems. And his tail swept away a third of the stars of heaven, and threw them to the earth* (Rev 12:3-4).

Satan rebelled against God and heaven. In a great battle, Michael and his forces drove him out. Not out of the spiritual dimension, but out of the place we know as heaven in the spiritual realm. At that time, he somehow took a third of the angels with him, whether willingly or unwillingly, we do not know.

Were a third of the angels co-conspirators? Did they fight to put him on the throne? There is no scriptural evidence that the swept angels are what we know as demons. But we know there are angels under his command, who fight on his behalf, like the prince of Persia mentioned in the Book of Daniel.

Jesus seems to know Satan well. When rebuking the Pharisees, he talks about *their* relationship to Satan.

You are of your father the devil, and you want to do the desires of your father. He was a murderer from the beginning, and does not stand in the truth, because there is no truth in him. Whenever he speaks a lie, he speaks from his own nature; for he is a liar, and the father of lies (John 8:44).

"A murderer from the beginning . . ." What is that about? We know there was a war, but what precipitated the fighting: Intrigue? Betrayal? Attempted coup? A murder? Appears so. Who is Satan? Apparently, he is a creature willing to kill anyone who stands in his way to greatness and self-deserved worship. I can imagine him whispering to Cain, egging him on into the murder of his brother, Abel. "Revenge is what's important here: Abel slighted you; he made you look little. You need to punish him. Pick up that rock. When he turns away—"

He who does what is sinful is of the devil, because the devil has been sinning from the beginning. The reason the Son of God appeared was to destroy the devil's work (1 John 3:8).

This is what I talked about earlier: that Jesus came to right the wrongs, to fix that which was broken (or those things which were broken). Something only he could do. Something only God could do.

The Bible does not specifically say Satan tempted Eve so she picked and ate of the forbidden fruit, although Ezekiel thinks he was there. We read that a deceitful serpent talked to her. The serpent may not have been the actual Satan, but he could have been if the serpent was a type of dragon. And if the serpent was not actually Satan, he certainly worked as a proxy, like the Beast in the Book of Revelation (Rev 13:1). The punishment for the serpent, that *"he will crush your head"* (Gen 3:15) seems to be a reference to Jesus defeating Satan at the resurrection. Therefore, even if the actual serpent was not Satan, the punishment of the surrogate fell on him. And I would suggest that we can call the serpent in the Garden, Satan or the devil, and still be quite accurate.

What creature is diametrically opposed to God and the restoration and reconciliation of the world's population? Whom do you think best fits into this category?

Satan is the embodiment of pure evil. When I say Pure Evil, some of you will think of horror movies and the scariest version of this idea: terrorism, murder, torture, violence.

But it includes much more: Those people who live by fear, cruelty, hubris, bullying, arrogance, pretense, and condescension are either puppets or willing subjects just because they enjoy these actions, this type of behavior, or somehow think it necessary in a twisted sort of way. Not all of these behaviors at once: I know people who specialize in one or two of these actions to the detriment of themselves and the people who have to be around them.

If you do not believe in Satan, you might as well be in this category, because your head is in the sand. Did this comment upset some of you? Ask yourself why. Do you believe the Bible? The Bible mentions this creature from the beginning to the end—Genesis to Revelation. Jesus and the apostles spoke of him and his ways. Satan deceives, lies, and misleads people; his key traits and abilities— modus operandi. Satan believes he can change the outcome—that the plan God set in place for this world can be broken and dismantled. Satan even believes he can change prophecy.

An angel came to Daniel in a dream and said, *"He will speak against the Most High and oppress his saints and try to change the set times and laws"* (Dan 7:25). There have always been rules in this conflict—laws—and whenever he can get away with it, Satan is a rule bender and regulation breaker.

But to Satan nothing is written in stone—nothing is sacred. He did not grudgingly agree to the rules—not at all. He circumvents the rules every chance he gets. To him everything has the potential for reversal or negation. Instead, we know that the Holy Spirit keeps him in check (restrains) until the End Times, when he will be allowed—for a short time—to exercise his full power against God's people and the world (2 Thess 2:6-12).

Isn't that a sign of an arrogant person? If he can stop or reverse what is supposed to happen, he can upset the laws that govern the world and God's plans. And when the Holy Spirit finally—at the perfectly planned moment—steps aside, worldwide destruction will surely follow. At the end of all things, the book of Revelation tells us that for a short time, Satan has unlimited power and authority on the earth, something he has not had before.

Then what happens?

And he performed great and miraculous signs, even causing fire to come down from heaven to earth in full view of everyone (Rev 13:13).

Sounds like he makes the evening news.

DRAGON'S

CHAPTER ELEVEN

AGENTS

SHAPE CHANGERS
AND DECEPTION

And no wonder, for Satan himself masquerades as an angel of light (2 Cor 11:14).

If you are a master of deception, well experienced and practiced in your craft, and you want to deceive a large group of people, just appear to someone as an angel, throw around a little "magic" and power, predict something that will happen, or perform a "miracle."

Do not let anyone who delights in false humility and the worship of angels disqualify you for the prize (Col 2:18).

Paul thought it was necessary to warn the church in Colossae against the worship of angels. At one point in John's vision, he fell down before the angel to worship him. The angel shouted:

Do not do it! I am a fellow servant with you and with your brothers the prophets and all who keep the words of this book. WORSHIP GOD! (Rev 22:8-9).

True angels of God are our brothers in arms.

Every Christmas we read stories of Gabriel talking to Mary, Joseph, Zechariah, and the shepherds, so we are already open to the idea of an angel appearing. But Gabriel always gave a message that was in line with the previous scriptures of the Bible—a continuity of purpose and style—as God's true representative. Gabriel would never tell anyone to create a book that was in direct contravention to the Bible. In the Biblical appearances, Gabriel's message did not contradict or negate previous Bible passages, but rather answered a question or gave us a prophecy: The virgin shall give birth, or the coming of the Messiah, or an answer to prayer—a quote from Isaiah 7:14.

Satan is most effective when producing something that sounds like the truth—a half-truth, in order to get a person nodding: "Yes, that sounds about right . . .", even if the outcome will be the opposite. I am thinking of the deceit he worked on Eve. Nothing has changed. He and his minions worked that way then and operate that way now, and we are their targets.

Speaking of the Beast and his power in the End Times, Paul wrote:

The coming of the lawless one will be in accordance with the work of Satan displayed in all kinds of counterfeit miracles, signs, and wonders, and in every sort of evil that deceives those who are perishing. They perish because they refused to love the truth and so be saved (2 Thess 2:9-10).

Do not be mistaken: Satan specifically designs these counterfeit miracles, signs, and wonders to deceive modern twenty-first century people. If it happened today, would the following miracle make you wonder?

When standing in front of Pharaoh, Moses told Aaron to throw his walking staff on the floor, and it turned into a writhing serpent. Did that shock the Pharaoh's priests? Not at all! They laughed and threw their own walking staffs down, which also turned into serpents (Exodus 7:9-12). Although Aaron's serpent-staff ate theirs, that is not the point. The point is that Satan and his followers have real power, and they use it to further their agenda—control, tyranny, destruction.

We see this when one person bullies another; when the stronger beats on the weak or powerless, abuses or harms innocent children, enslaves others, persecutes someone who believes differently, maltreats animals, and uses pornography in all its forms. The list is endless. By this savagery, people are acting out Satan's agenda. Some are sociopathic and enjoy the violence. Others blindly follow and obey the leaders, no matter how outrageous the demands. Sounds like Islamic extremism, doesn't it? They use a few verses in the Quran to justify their wretched and evil actions—a book given to a man by an angel—supposedly Gabriel (Quran 53:4–9). Go figure.

Do you remember the verse prior, where Jesus said the Pharisees were acting like their father the devil? (John 8:44–45). You do not have to kill black cats, drink blood, and worship Satan in a dark, smoky temple to be his follower and child. Satan craves worship and will take it in any form he can. He tempted Jesus that way and he tempts us the same—all the time.

The god of this age has blinded the minds of unbelievers, so that they cannot see the Light of the Gospel of the glory of Christ, who is the image of God (2 Corinthians 4:4).

How has the god of this age, Satan, blinded people?

I have found that if people choose to not believe something like the Gospel, they will blindly and willingly follow a lie, if there is even a miniscule shred of truth to it, and especially if it is entertaining. Hitler put on a big show, touting Germanic exceptionalism and most of the country lined up behind him. Those who challenged him and did not emigrate—ref. to Dietrich Bonhoeffer—died. I think we would all agree that Hitler was a tool in Satan's hand.

Jesus healed the sick, healed a man born blind, and even raised the dead. What was the Jerusalem leadership's response to these unheard of miracles? John tells us Lazarus was dead for four days *and stinking* (John 11:39). Jesus wept and then called him out of the tomb. The Pharisees were so angered by the raising of Lazarus, they conspired to kill Jesus *and Lazarus* (John 11:53, 12:9-11). What happened to Jesus a short time later? Crucified like a common criminal.

Most folks like a good magic show. I enjoy slight of hand, close-up magic, misdirection. In the End Times, Satan will come with miracles also, but these miracles will amaze, baffle, and impress. These miracles will astonish a worldwide audience, bringing glory to the performer. The Satan miracles will point people to him. "Isn't he wonderful!" people will proclaim, clapping excitedly, especially when he causes fire to fall down from heaven (Rev 13:13) and brings a great statue to life (Rev 13:15). A world of brilliant people will be impressed, and what happens next? We read that for all practical purposes, these smart "modern" and enlightened folks follow the Beast and worship the Dragon (Rev 13:3–4).

I am not surprised. Most people are not overtly worshiping Satan, but they worship him by obeying the proxy—the Beast—doing what he tells them to do while ignoring their conscience, and God. In this case, inaction is just as bad as action for the wrong side.

Has anything like this happened already in the world? Absolutely.

But even if we or an angel from heaven should preach a gospel other than the one we preached to you, let him be eternally condemned! (Galatians 1:8).

Paul is emphatic—a warning to believers to be on their guard, because things like this happen—angels preaching. The Church of Galatia was *"thrown into confusion"* (Gal 1:7) by something or someone, and Paul goes to great lengths in his letter to re-explain who he is and what the Gospel is all about. Some of the greatest passages in the Bible are there: the Fruit of the Spirit, and *"The only thing that counts is faith expressing itself through love"* (Gal 5:6).

There are many examples of an angel speaking to humans, giving false messages, some with tragic consequences. I alluded to one, here is another.

LOURDES, FRANCE

In 1858, a peasant girl, Bernadette Soubirous, on the way with two friends to gather wood, saw something: a vision at the Massabielle Grotto. When I read the story, a few things made me suspicious.

1. She described the apparition as a beautiful lady, who looked *exactly like the Blessed Virgin statue in the church.*[1] If the creature were actually Mary, the mother of Jesus, she would not appear EXACTLY as a statue created from the imagination of an artist.

2. During one visit by the creature, a man came by, whistling and probing around the grotto with a stick. Bernadette described the event as an attack on the lady. Although he could not see the lady, himself, his stick accidentally tapped against her ankles and she recoiled. "'Go away!' Bernadette's voice was piercing. 'You're hurting the lady. And her feelings, too,' she cried."[2] If this were really Mary appearing to a young girl, the probing stick of an old man would not cause fear and pain. I wonder what it was about his stick and his attitude that bothered the creature.

3. The creature's most disturbing visitation to Bernadette came with the sounds of fighting and warning. During the vision, Bernadette heard someone shouting: "Once more the piercing cries arose, 'Flee, flee—Avaunt from here!' The lady's face was described as stern and proud. With wrinkled brow, she looked attentively at the river (where the fighting sounds came from), as though to tame it with her eyes radiant blue. The uproar yielded at once. The hoarse voices crashed into silence."[3] I believe this event was God's angels fighting Satan's angels, with one or more of God's angels warning Bernadette to run away from the creature: spiritual warfare, real and deadly, heard this time but not seen.

4. Over a period of a year, this creature appeared to Bernadette. Nearly each time the girl asked for its name. At the last appearance, Bernadette asked a final time, and it said, "I am the immaculate conception."[4]

Investigators wondered that the lady did not say she was immaculately conceived. Instead, she said she was THE Immaculate Conception—perfectly conceived from the beginning. We could describe a certain dragon that way.

Four years before, in 1854, to promote the worship of Mary as a deity *equal with God* (who does this remind you of?), Pope Pius IX suggested that Mary's father conceived her in her mother's womb, but God intervened. God kept Mary immaculate—spotlessly clean, pure, without original sin (as passed down from Adam like all other humans—see Romans 5:12 for sin of Adam)—at the time of conception. The idea was to free Mary from original sin and personal sin—elevating her high above normal humans. The doctrine teaches that Mary became sinless by the work of Jesus, but by a retroactive application to her case, making her always sinless. This is a convoluted argument with no biblical bases whatsoever—unscriptural nonsense. The creature in the grotto turned this false doctrine on its ear, by appropriating the idea to itself—with a twist, of course.

Catholic bishops promoted and perpetuated this heretical doctrine by granting popes the power to proclaim infallible doctrine, even if it contradicted the Bible. The result is a sinless Mary, now referred to as the Queen of Heaven, making her equal with Christ and God. People pray to her rather than God, because she is supposed to be more accessible or more sympathetic.

Is it wrong to worship and pray to Mary instead of God? I told a Catholic friend of mine that I only prayed to God, and he said that Mary had appeared to people all over the world, so it must be okay to pray to her. If we are supposed to be praying to God and we direct our prayers somewhere else, would that mean they are ineffective? I would imagine so. It would be a form of idolatry.

There are too many scriptures to list here about praying to God only, but when John tried to worship the angel in Revelation 19:10 and 22:9, the angel shouted, *"Worship God!"* which includes our prayers and supplications. At no time does the Bible suggest that we should pray or talk to someone or something other than God.

Interestingly, Catholics are not required to believe these revelations from Lourdes. However, the worship of Mary as a perpetual virgin, who was not born like humans but immaculately conceived by God, equal with God, continues.

Now thousands of people go to the grotto every year, hoping to be healed—*and some are.* If people are healed by the water, does that automatically mean God is there and approving? No. The dark side also performs miracles, like the Egyptian priests: It is still a deception.

Dear friends, do not believe every spirit, but test the spirits to see whether they are from God . . . (1 John 4:1).

That statement was true when John wrote it and it is true today: Even now spirits need to be tested.

The Bible tells us that Jesus was not a pretty man, that we should not desire him just based on his looks (Isaiah 53:2). So I am convinced that when the Beast comes to rule the world in the End Times—our near future, he will probably be handsome. Why? Because he will be the opposite of Christ—anti-Christ. Some people will believe his corrupt announcements because the anti-Christ (a.k.a. the Beast) will look like the kind of person to deliver a truthful-sounding message, or he will say those things that people greatly desire to hear (2 Tim 4:3). They will forgive the lapses and discrepancies in his character and controversial comments, because he will look good, sound smart, and will tap into something we were already thinking or worrying about. If he makes sense on some point, and we start nodding in agreement with the truthful part, we are in danger of continuing to nod approvingly when the message subtly deviates to the half-truth, the lying part. The Bible tells us that everyone, everywhere, will greatly admire the Beast (Rev 13:8). For example, I know people who voted for Mitt Romney when he ran for president just based on his looks (No, I do not think Mitt is the anti-Christ).

The Spirit clearly says that in the latter times some will abandon the faith and follow deceiving spirits and things taught by demons (1 Tim 4:1).

How can someone who really believes in God, turn away from the faith and follow something else? The deception must be exceptionally powerful. But do not be fooled. Jesus talked about this: false prophets, false Christs, those promoting a different gospel or a different bible. Some will even perform miracles as they subtly turn believers away from God (Matt 24:24; 2 Cor 11:13-15).

If CNN highlighted someone proclaiming to work on God's behalf, causing fire to fall from heaven, devouring our enemies, would you automatically believe whatever they proclaimed? Many will. Some will nominate him for sainthood while he is still alive. He will certainly be promoted as a world leader. People will line up in droves to praise him and get a selfie, while watching the replay on CNN and Youtube until their eyes bug out.

Who is the anti-Christ?

Satan brings about the end of our world by giving his power to a human being, which apparently must be a rule he cannot violate—instead of coming himself. I mean, it seems he has the ability to appear temporarily as the spiritual creature of his choosing—angel, young woman—to certain people, but to walk the earth as a human requires a human body.

The Dragon gave the Beast his power and his throne and great authority (Rev 13:2).

Power, throne, authority. That is pretty much everything. Perhaps this is how Satan used the serpent to deceive Eve. The whole world will follow this guy, who seems to recover miraculously from a fatal head wound (Rev 13:3). There is something to watch for. Someone of great political or religious importance (or both), recovering from what appears to be a shot to the head. Wait. How can Satan use this person if a high-powered bullet punctures the brain?

Jude's letter gives us a clue.

But even the archangel Michael, when he was disputing with the devil about the body of Moses, did not dare to bring a slanderous accusation against him, but said, "The LORD rebuke you!" (Jude 1:9).

Because he struck the rock (God told Moses to only speak to the rock—a type and shadow of Jesus—Num 20:6–12; 1 Cor 10:4), God did not allow Moses to enter the Promised Land. Instead, he climbed Mount Nebo as God instructed him, and died (Deut 32:49–52). Satan knew that if he possessed the body and controlled it, he could ruin God's plans for the Israelites in the Promised Land. The Archangel Michael would not let that happen. If Satan controlled the dead body of Moses, would that make Moses a zombie? Probably. I do not think God likes zombies.

So Satan will possess the body of someone great, who apparently died by assassination (Rev 13:3, 12–14). That at the moment of death, Satan will enter the lifeless body, bringing it back to life with all of his diabolic power, malice, and horror. If the Beast was already someone we idolized and followed, how much more will everyone rejoice over the miraculous recovery, while the actual man we revered will be long gone. In his place will be the presence of absolute unrestrained evil. Now, instead of trying to lead Israel astray, Satan will focus his energy on destroying the whole world. Just being in the same room with this "person" will be scary to many.

Aren't dragons just fun?

SOUL

CHAPTER TWELVE

CATCHERS

DEMON POSSESSION

Is this why Satan thought he could sub-plant God, because he had the ability to create certain creatures? I can hear him shout, "It's alive! It's alive! I am a god! I create living things!"

I have wondered if Satan has creative powers, which he uses regularly—without permission, of course, circumventing the established laws. For example, what are demons? Are they fallen angels, or something else? They seem to be spiritual parasites, a creature designed to infiltrate and take over the human form, and sometimes animals, forcing some people to perform strange and bizarre acts, either against their will, or by influencing the mind so they do the wrong thing anyhow.

In the Gospel of Luke, we read about a physically powerful man who lived in a cemetery, not wearing clothes. The villagers feared him greatly, because even chains could not hold him. The villagers believed he was full of devils. The title for this passage in my Bible says, *"The Healing of the Demon-possessed Man"* (Luke 8:26-39).

When Jesus stepped out of the boat, the deranged man was already on the shore, waiting. He knew who Jesus was. Jesus commanded the demons to come out of him. Instead, he ran and fell at Jesus' feet, crying, *"What do you want with me, Jesus, Son of the Most High God? I beg you, do not torture me!"*

I find it most interesting that, at Jesus' command to depart (Luke 8:29), this swarm of demons *did not* immediately come out of the man. Instead, they initiated a conversation, which moves to a compromise.

"What is your name?" Jesus asked.

"Legion," the man replied, *"because we are many. Do not send us into the Abyss. Send us into the pigs."*

According to the demons, Jesus probably had the ability to send them to the Abyss, right then, which they greatly feared. But also because, as parasites, they lived vicariously through their victim (similar to what I said Satan wanted to do—take over a body). They knew the gig was up with the poor fellow they occupied. Did the legion of demons gain something by soul leeching their human host? Were they able to feed on that life, imperfect as it was?

Jesus gave them permission to go into the pigs, which then ran down the hill into the lake and drowned. What was that about? Did the demons drive the pigs crazy, killing themselves? Or, did the demons always see this option as temporary, and when free of the pigs, they would move on to their preferable type of victim—a human host? Sounds like the horror film *The Body Snatchers* (1956, 1993), doesn't it?

We know the people were Samaritans, because they ate pork, something God forbid the Jews to do. By destroying the herd of pigs, the demons actually won three points: They destroyed a major source of food, so that the people begged Jesus to leave; he was hard on their economy. In addition, the pig incident hampered his ministry greatly due to his untimely departure. Finally, the demons apparently escaped.

When the villagers arrived, they found the man sitting at the feet of Jesus *". . . clothed and in his right mind."*

I have wondered about demon possession. Horror movies exploit the subject for profit, while modern-thinking people dismiss the idea as mythology and delusion. Although demon possession sounds commonplace in the New Testament, the scientifically oriented person seeks a rational, medical, or psychological explanation.

How would you define demon possession? In one sense it is an invasion of our physical bodies, hence we read in the Bible of demons being cast out—of the body.

But what is actually happening inside the body with our spirit? I have wondered if demons cling to our spiritual self, thereby appearing to possess the body, while suffocating, debilitating, weighing us down—the old "monkey on the back" concept: attacking our spirit with physical harm and words, strangling, biting, and stinging, which then spill over into our physical world with aches, pains, mental issues, and problem behaviors.

What I am saying is that there is demon possession and then there is demon oppression. Demon oppression would be an assault on our spiritual person, which might be more common among people, even pervasive. Something we suspect but seem to have little control over.

In the Gospel of Luke, Jesus sent out the disciples to share the Good News and heal the sick (Luke 10:1-17). They returned in great excitement, exclaiming, *"Lord, even the demons submit to us in your name."*

Jesus' response is interesting. He tells them that he saw Satan fall like lightning from heaven, meaning their work seriously affected Satan. Then to illustrate the idea of Satan being disabled, Jesus says he gave the disciples *authority to trample on snakes and scorpions* (Luke 10:19). Odd phrasing. What could Jesus really mean here?

I realized Jesus was describing *how* demons operate in spiritual attacks, spiritual oppression. They squeeze and sting our spirits, affecting our bodies and minds. The stings are pointed attacks that create aches and pains. If we could see these spiritual attacks, I believe we would see stingers penetrating the spiritual version of our bodies at various places, while causing all manner of physical and mental ailments.

What happens when a snake wraps around its victim? The squeezing brings a sense of suffocation, a broken body and spirit, which I see revealed in our bodies as depression, discouragement, melancholy, and anxiety.

Are demonic attacks responsible for all physical and mental issues? Of course not, but we would benefit by knowing, understanding, and studying this subject.

What can we do about these types of attacks? Let us take our lesson from the disciples. *"Lord, even the demons submit to us in your name."* The name of Jesus is a powerful source of help in the area of spiritual warfare. And remember, we can use scripture to fight Satanic attacks.

Is prayer helpful? Several scriptures tell us it is.

Jesus told Peter:

Simon, Simon, Satan has asked to sift you [all] as wheat. But I have prayed for you, Simon, that your faith may not fail. And when you have turned back, strengthen your brothers (Luke 22:31-32).

The key here is that the spiritual attack will not prove fatal *because Jesus prayed for him,* although Peter felt terrible by the time it was all done—betraying Christ, denying him three times. In some Christian circles, when people feel like they are under spiritual attack, they go to prayer and get help from others in prayer. And I know for a fact that it works.

THE ROLE OF PRAYER

I know God wants an ongoing conversation with us, like anyone in a relationship: not just running to him every time we have a need, although he will not turn you away then either. Something is better than nothing, but we need to know how to pray.

When people ask me how to pray, I send them to the Psalms. David is still a great teacher. In the Psalms you will learn to pray, because when you read the Psalms, you are reading prayers and prophecies that David (and others) put to music, revealing the heart of David. However, you will also learn something about the heart of God, what his desires and expectations are for us. With David as the example, we study his intimate relationship and seek to emulate him. How do we do that?

I take the prayers and make them my own—personalized. Let's use Psalm 1 as an example.

Verse 1: *"Blessed is the man who does not walk in the counsel of the wicked,"* or, Joel will be blessed when he does not take advice from mean and dishonest people.

Verse 2: *"But his delight is in the law of the LORD, and on his law he meditates day and night,"* or, Joel delights in God's Word, reading and thinking about it often.

Verse 3: *"He is like a tree planted by streams of water, which yields its fruit in season and whose leaf does not wither. Whatever he does prospers,"* or, Joel is like a tree (upright, with deep roots, nourished), and his life produces fruit, prospering in life and relations.

Verse 6, "For the LORD watches over Joel—"

Psalm 3 rewritten as my own.

Verse 1 and following: *"O LORD, how many are my foes!"* or, O LORD, how many are *my problems!* How many problems rise up against me—illness, guilt, regrets, sorrow, loss, anxiety. People say you will help me. But you, O God, are a shield of protection and love around me, my Glorious One, who lifts up my sad head. To you, O LORD, I cry aloud, and you answer me from heaven. I lie down and sleep; I wake again, because you O LORD sustain and make me strong and able. I will not fear the many problems and issues that come against me on every side.

Look at each Psalm and personalize it for yourself. David had enemies. Who or what are yours—illness, strained or broken relations, pains, anxieties, temptations, heartache, guilt, regrets, fear? In this way, you can make the Psalms come alive in your heart and life, and you will come to understand how both David and Jesus approached their relationship to God, as father *and friend*. When you sit down with your Bible and consider how you fit into each Psalm like this, and what it means for you personally, you are meditating on the scriptures.

Why did I mention Jesus here? Take a moment to read Psalm 22. Who do you think is actually speaking? Like Isaiah and other prophets, David, under the inspiration of the Holy Spirit, prophesied about Jesus in the future. Psalm 22:1:

My God, my God, why have you forsaken me? They pierced my hands and my feet. They divided my garments among them and cast lots for my clothing (Psalm 22:1, 16, 18).

At times, God speaks directly to me in the Psalms. Look at how I changed a few words starting in Psalm 32:8.

Dear Joel, I will instruct you and teach you in the way you should go; I will counsel you and watch over you. Oh Joel, do not be like the horse or the mule, which have no understanding and must be controlled by bit and bridle, or they will not come to you. Many are the problems of the wrong doers, but my unfailing love surrounds you, Joel, because you trust in me.

I have many other examples, but let me encourage everyone interested in prayer, while learning to hear God's voice, to study the Psalms and apply them, personally, like this to their lives. Find your favorite Psalm: mine is Psalm 139.

After Satan departed, we read that angels came to minister to Jesus (Matt 4:11). The writer of Hebrews wrote that angels are ministering spirits sent to serve believers (Heb 1:14). Would the angels be more responsive and helpful if we just prayed, asking for help from God and any agents he sent to assist or deliver? They are on the inside—the spiritual side—able to see what we only suspect.

When we read in the Bible about the things some people do when demon-possessed—acting strange, falling down with foaming mouth—the enlightened mind automatically goes to mental illness or some other known problem in the Diagnostic and Statistical Manual of Mental Disorders (a.k.a. the DSM). But if it was only mental illness or something like epilepsy, then why did the demons speak, calling Jesus the Son of God, or negotiating their fate when about to be cast out?

The answer is that two things are going on: mental illness *and* demon possession. The line between the two is often blurred. When a demon possesses a human, it looks and acts like a mental sickness. Why? Because demon possession makes us sick. It is like having a virus in our soul—a spiritual leech or parasite—abnormal, unnatural.

Does that mean that all mental illness is demon possession or oppression in one form or another? Of course not, just like all sickness is not cancer. However, before you casually cast off this notion of demon possession, agree with me that something is going on here that we do not fully understand.

I wish we had a scientific instrument that would show us a spiritual possession or attack—a Spiritual Viewer. Some of you will remind me that the Bible serves that purpose and some people have gifts of discernment and healing. I know.

But the attacks are so widespread and pervasive, and the Church seems so impotent at times. For the whole Church to really have the ability to help the mentally ill, neurotic, disturbed, and troubled minds, it would require a great outpouring of the Holy Spirit. As the pastor of a church, I was constantly praying for people suffering from all sorts of mental instabilities—simple to profound: some we could help, some not so much. In the meantime, the world is reeling.

How do we explain the many mass shootings, attacks on children, terrorisms, hateful extremisms? Satan is happy to let the modern-thinking person "poo poo" the idea of demons as mythological and religious flimflam. Being invisible and dismissed as Christian hokeyism is Satan's best disguise. The ostrich head in the sand syndrome; if I do not see it, it does not exist. Or, if I can't measure it, it is irrelevant.

Is there better proof of Satan's interference? Yes. Isaiah 65:20 tells us that when Satan is unable to interfere—not free on the earth to do as he pleases—people will live much longer and happier lives. *"He who dies at a hundred will be thought a mere youth."* This is a profound difference. It makes you wonder how Satan hinders and obstructs all portions of our lives today.

Comedian Flip Wilson said, "The devil made me do it!"

In the Garden, Eve said, "The serpent made me do it!"

And so it goes.

The old dragon is probably responsible for much of what we call mental illness, whether demon possession or not. His agents are subtle, speaking to us, tweaking our thoughts, and maneuvering our feelings for their ends.

And what are those ends?

Anything that distracts us from God, anything that creates doubt and confusion, anything that supports his side of the war through wrongdoing, misdirection, and bafflement. Didn't we just read that Satan would use the Beast to perform great miracles and lead the whole world astray? If he calls fire down on our enemies (real or perceived), everyone will rejoice.

We read in 1 Chronicles 21:1 that *"Satan rose up against Israel and incited David to take a census of Israel."* That can only mean Satan put the idea into David's head, and David acted on the idea, knowing it was wrong.

How does that work?

Have you ever said or done something you instantly regretted? Have you ever had a strange or evil thought come into your head that conflicted with your moral and ethical underpinnings? Have you ever been doing something completely innocuous and had an evil thought enter your mind that was the total opposite of the person you really are? Have you ever dwelled on a revenge you wished to initiate, a glory or riches you wished to receive, what you would do if you won the lottery? Have you ever found yourself reviewing and replaying those failures in your life, where you said or did something shameful and regretful, where you were hurt or shamed, or did that to someone else? Did you ever drink or take drugs, which caused you to act and speak in a way that was in stark contrast to the person you really are—most of the time?

If you can answer "yes" to any of these questions, you have suffered from an outside influence; not in every case, of course, but more often than we know or realize.

A skeptic will say that our own proclivities toward the dark side cause these types of thoughts and inner talk to happen in our heads. I agree, to a point. But I am also convinced that Satan, via his agents, can and will steer our mind down these dark alleys, so you will wallow in guilt and shame, get into trouble, ruin relations, perhaps become paralyzed in your thinking and actions, or at a minimum become less effective in whatever good you are doing, especially if that good benefits others. Your choices are at stake. By appealing to your pride and sense of self-interest, you hover between the choices that can change your very destiny.

To put it simply, Satan wants you to fail.

Peter experienced this first hand.

In Matthew 16:16-23 we read that Peter confesses Jesus as *"the Messiah, Son of the Living God."* Jesus praises Peter for this wonderful, God-inspired insight and tells everyone Peter will lead the Church. Hurray for Peter!

Then what happens? Jesus tells them he must go to Jerusalem to suffer and die— referring to his necessary death on the cross. Peter, probably filled with his own self-importance because of the praise he just received, takes Jesus aside and firmly rebukes him, saying it will never happen; he will not die like this, not on Peter's watch.

Jesus turns on him in a snap, shouting:

Out of my sight, Satan! You are a stumbling block to me; you do not have in mind the things of God, but the things of men! (Matt 16:23).

Poor Peter.

He rose to the highest heights one minute and quickly fell to the lowest depths the next. In an instant. Shock and horror must have been written all over his face. I can see the other disciples cringe, moving away from him, out of the blast radius.

Who put that thought in Peter's head? A simple idea that sounds rational, sensible, and helpful—even enlightened? Satan. Peter's righteous intent was to do a good deed, helping his friend—the Messiah—but he was completely out of step with God's plan and purpose.

Satan puts ideas in our head, whispering. "I'm important now; I know what's better for you than you do." Doesn't that sound like more prideful thinking, tripping over our tongue? Someone once said that the road to hell was paved in good intentions: those ideas we meant to work on, and those we did work on but for the wrong reasons.

THE PLACE OF FORGIVENESS

You might be thinking that I am off target with this chapter. It is about Demon Possession after all, and I have managed to talk about prayer and now forgiveness. My purpose in wandering down these side paths is to talk about how to fight and defeat the enemy. Prayer might seem rather obvious to believers, but perhaps not so much forgiveness, which is why I wanted to spend a few pages on it.

I have heard people shout, "I will not forgive him! He hurt me, and I will not forgive until he apologizes—maybe not even then. I am right in this matter, and he is the wrongdoer."

Appealing to our pride, our righteous indignation, our innate sense of right and wrong, Satan manipulates us like stringed puppets. The problem is that forgiveness is necessary, whether the other person—the offender—realizes it or not. Forgiveness begins the healing in our wounded hearts. If reconciliation is possible, all the better, but it is not a foregone conclusion. Jesus told Peter to forgive sacrificially (Matt 18:22), which goes along—hand in hand—with our need to love sacrificially (1 Cor 13).

Satan would rather that you harden your heart and stand your ground than give way to forgiveness and love, whether right or wrong. What is even worse, some people withhold forgiveness, because they know it is hurting the other person. We call that revenge or vindictiveness—an eye for an eye—I suffered; now you will suffer. Have a nice day!

Recently, I had a guy call me one evening out of the clear blue—from another state— who I had not seen or talked to in more than a year. I barely knew him. As soon as I remembered who he was, he announced that he was forgiving me. I asked what about. He told me I said something that really upset him. Again, I did not remember the specifics. He told me. It still did not register, at first.

Reflecting on that distant and brief conversation, I realized something went wrong: He came to me the year before to confess to serious past sins and troubling behavior. A question from me sent him reeling. Although his outward demeanor had not changed, the formal confession was actually over right there. The question I asked him ate away at his soul, until he decided to call everyone who ever upset him, ever, and tell them he forgave them. The twist on this story is that this is not how forgiveness works.

Forgiveness is not about calling people and rubbing their noses in perceived sins from your point of view. True forgiveness is about you talking to God, who brings inner healing and reconciliation. You do not have to see or talk to the person who hurt you, which is why you can receive the comfort of forgiveness even though someone died, or you can't talk to someone, or you don't particularly want to see or talk to them (someone in prison possibly). Instead of calling people, and in this tangential way rebuking them (which makes you feel better, getting it off your chest), it is God who works inside you to bring true and lasting healing.

In this case, he felt like a victim and wanted me to be sure I felt like the perpetrator, even if I did not—and still do not. However, I did feel like a victim afterward. Nevertheless, I took it to God and forgave him.

How do you love and forgive sacrificially when you either do not want to, or feel unable to? On our own strength, true and complete forgiveness is nearly impossible—I know. But if we take it to God, asking him to lead and direct us in this matter, we will be successful. Pray. Humble yourself and tell God you are trying:

Father in heaven, I need your help and intervention in this matter—I know I must forgive, I am saying the words, but my heart is not in it—my heart needs to be transformed.

We all have regrets and shame for actions done and words spoken in our past. I will be completely minding my own business and rotten kinds of thoughts or regretful situations will enter my mind from long ago. And it doesn't matter how far in the past it happened. I will ask, Why am I thinking of this now? What made me think of that?

I met with a 96-year-old man who said he had no regrets. Really? I did not believe it, partly because I had known him all my life and could count off regrettable scenes from memory. If you do not have regrets, then you must be living a perfect life so your friends and family praise the very thought of you. Or perhaps it is a life ending in some kind of denial. But if he really reconciled all of his regrets, so his heart and mind were at peace, then I am thankful.

So there is a sense that we must also forgive ourselves for past mistakes. Just as mentioned earlier, pray to God and ask him to bury the past, forgive completely, absolutely. He promises that when we do this, our failures and wrongdoing will *"be remembered no more"* (Heb 8:12, 10:17).

I, even I, am he who blots out your transgressions for my own sake, and I will not remember your sins (failures, wrongdoing—Isaiah 43:25).

I ask for forgiveness, healing, and guidance. A clear conscience. Hope. For help to have better conduct in the future, learning from mistakes. Trying. All things the devil is opposed to, but ours to appropriate by faith. But more than that, more than just faith, because God enables us to be successful. He really intervenes.

When I say we appropriate it by faith, it sounds like we will get better with positive thinking. Let me say instead: trust God. When we turn difficult things over to him, like forgiveness of those who have wronged us or forgiveness of ourselves, he does not just work on our mind, he works on our heart also. An inner transformation takes place.

That might sound confusing—the distinction between heart and mind. What I mean is that our brain, our mind, is the thinking part and the heart is the emotional part. There is evidence of something going on in this area when heart transplant patients begin to feel things that were once familiar to the heart donor.

Paul became a believer after Jesus died. As a Pharisee, he persecuted Christians and approved the stoning of Stephen (Acts 7). This bothered him his whole life.

I am the least of the apostles and do not even deserve to be called an apostle, because I persecuted the church of God (1 Cor 15:9).

But look how he follows up this confession and admission of guilt.

But by the grace of God I am what I am, and his grace to me was not without effect. No, I worked harder than all of them, yet not I, but the grace of God that was with me (vs 10).

Paul learned something about grace and forgiveness, and he tells us how to do it in his letter to the Romans.

In view of God's mercy, offer your bodies as living sacrifices, holy and pleasing to God—which is your spiritual worship. Do not conform any longer to the pattern of this world, but be transformed by the renewing of your mind (Romans 12:1-2, also Romans 8:29; 2 Cor 3:18).

God is merciful. Full of grace and forgiveness. When we turn to him, he immediately reaches out to us, like when Peter sank below the waves while walking on the water with Jesus (Matt 14:30-31).

What does it mean to offer ourselves as a living sacrifice?

In the Old Testament Jewish sacrifice, as explained by God, the priest took a certain type of animal, slew it on the altar, and burned it up. The sacrifice was to please God and gain personal forgiveness.

What Paul is telling us to do, what he learns for himself, is to present ourselves to God, holding nothing back, like a lamb for the slaughter, absolutely. Paul tells us that it is a form of worship to trust God like this—without reservation. Then Paul says something I did not understand for a long time: *"be transformed by the renewing of your mind."*

Here is the problem: If I could simply use my mind to fix the problems in my life and be a better person, I would not really need God, would I? But no one can; we all fall short. Finally, while standing in the shower one morning, the answer came to me. The Holy Spirit does the transforming. The Holy Spirit renews the heart and mind, but we need to ask for and allow it. By laying our *selves* down, in humility, asking God to intervene in our lives, giving up our control, the transformation begins. God's effort inside. The Holy Spirit's transforming work, not mine.

How does this work?

When I finally understood the concept, I prayed, "Father in Heaven, with all my heart and mind, I lay down my life before you, asking you to intervene by the power of your Holy Spirit; transform my heart and mind into your image. Amen."

And do you know what happened? *Nothing*.

But each day I kept praying the same way (yes, I often pray in the shower).

Two weeks later, I was driving north on Interstate 5 near Fort Lewis (now Joint Base Lewis-McChord). It was raining a little, traffic was tight across the three lanes, and I was in the middle. Suddenly, the car on the left swerved into my lane. That was bad, but then he hit the brakes. I jammed on my brakes, while glancing in the mirror to see if the person behind me could slow in time, and veered to the left. A near accident, but we survived. My passenger was freaking out, but I was calm. I was calm? I mean, I was wondering if the other person was having a medical emergency, or had missed their exit, or what. Then I wondered at this unusual calmness, and a thought came into my head: *You are being transformed from the inside out.*

There was no time for me to buck up and be calm in the crisis; I was just unusually calm as the crisis unfolded. Made all the more profound by my passenger's reaction, which would have been typical of me a few weeks earlier. What changed? The Holy Spirit was working on me from the inside out, *as promised.*

Why did it take two weeks to start seeing evidence of this work? Perhaps because I needed more work than others. Maybe some of you will see the Holy Spirit's results right away, because there is less of a mess to clean up.

But let me warn you, God is a gentleman. If you do not invite him to intervene in your life, he will let you continue to manage alone. However, if you pray like this, inviting him to transform you from the inside out, amazing things will happen. Again, this is not the power of positive thinking. Good things often come from positive thinking, but this is something else. Purposefully put your life into his hands. And don't do it just one time. Ephesians 4:23 tells us that this renewal is a daily affair ("*made new*" has a daily connotation in the Greek). I have to keep praying, telling God that I need this continuous intervention and transformation in my life. I am a work in progress, like all of us. Some days are great, some not so.

The liturgical churches follow a church calendar. As I write this piece, we are entering the season of Lent, a time of self-examination, repentance, fasting, and prayer, leading up to Easter. I review how my year has gone, examining my spiritual growth or backsliding behaviors, and prayerfully determine how to continue.

SUMMARY

If you feel like you are under spiritual attack or influence, as evidenced by feelings, thoughts, and words you do not normally experience, resist Satan. Pray. Ask God to get involved. In those areas of your life that make you vulnerable, like unforgiveness, ask God to transform you from the inside out, so you become a stronger and better person. And enlist the aide of like-minded folks at your church.

FIGHTING

═══ CHAPTER THIRTEEN ═══

DRAGONS

TEMPTATION

Jesus went into the wilderness to be tempted by Satan. How did Satan tempt him? By showing him things. He did not need to "take" Jesus anywhere. He just needed to work on his mind, offering him power and authority in exchange for worldly trinkets (Matt 4:1-11). Nothing has changed. Satan puts ideas in our minds, and either we dwell on them, act on them, or we do not.

Can the Bible help us in the area of temptation?

How did Jesus battle Satan at that time and what can we learn from his successful trial? He used scripture. But so did Satan.

If you are the Son of God, tell these stones to become bread (Matt 4:3).

Satan got the title right—"THE Son of God," but he believed Jesus had pride like everyone else he had ever encountered. He was wrong. By the wording of his challenges, we see he still did not understand that part about Jesus—the incarnation, and the fact that the sin of Adam was not inside him. But he did understand that if Jesus misused his power, his mission would fail. So he says, if you are the Son of God prove it. Give me a demonstration of your power—show off a little.

Satan assumed that Jesus was hungry after fasting forty days, so he designed the first temptation to go right to his stomach; a common area of weakness in many people. Satan was right—as the Son of God, Jesus did have the ability to change rocks into bread. Then Jesus would have used his great power for his own selfish interests: an act of pride. If he gave in to this first temptation, he would fail in his mission as the Messiah, who came to serve others, not himself (Matt 20:28).

Jesus answered with scripture:

It is written: "Man does not live by bread alone, but on every word that comes from the mouth of God" (Deut 8:3).

That was the perfect scripture, because it referred to another test, where God allowed the Israelites to hunger in the wilderness and then gave them manna from heaven, *"to teach you that man does not live by bread alone . . ."* We read that after these three temptations, the angels came to help, and I wonder if they fed him manna.

Unlike the Israelites in the wilderness with Moses, who suffered for their unbelief and lack of faith, Jesus overcomes all hardship: *"Be of good cheer; I have overcome the world"* (John 16:33). Jesus told us manna was a type and shadow of himself, when he described himself as the Bread of Life (John 6:25–59). These verses and statements encourage and help us to be victorious over the world and Satan.

Satan was just getting started. He took Jesus to the peak of the Great Temple in Jerusalem, and said:

If you are the Son of God, throw yourself down. For it is written: "He will command his angels concerning you, and they will lift you up in their hands, so that you will not strike your foot against a stone" (Psalm 91:11-12).

Again, Satan acknowledges that Jesus is the Messiah, and appeals to his pride. Just as he tempted Eve, he uses the sayings of God, but with a deadly twist. I do not believe Jesus stood on the pinnacle of the Great Temple. If Jesus threw himself off the Temple, even mentally and not physically, the result would be the same—failure—because *in his mind, he had already chosen to do the wrong thing.*

Does it matter if you just ponder wrongful notions, or think something selfish, or dwell on a prideful thought with your mind? Is it sinful to imagine something wicked, naughty, or disgraceful just with your mind, if you do not act on it, or do not actually intend to act on it? The short answer is YES.

Jesus tried to explain this idea during his Sermon on the Mount talk. He said:

You have heard that it was said, "Do not commit adultery." But I tell you that anyone who looks at a woman lustfully has already committed adultery with her in his heart (Matt 5:27-28).

Busted!

Your heart and your mind are the battlefield, where you stand or fall. That is why secret sin, like viewing pornography on a home computer or phone, is still wrong.

Back to the Temple peak.

Jesus quickly answered:

It is also written: "Do not put the LORD your God to the test" (Deut 6:16).

Jesus does not argue or try to reason with Satan. He quotes scripture and lets it stand. *And scripture is always sufficient.*

Satan knows Jesus is the Messiah, the Son of God. But if Jesus is a also human, then Satan believes he must have the usual human weaknesses, all rooted in pride (like us). These temptations are based on selfish needs—food for the self-centered, wealth for the ego-centered, and self-determination instead of following God's will. One last test remains.

The first two temptations were crisis driven: alleviating hunger or God's intervention in a manufactured danger. Now Satan makes his final offer: fabulous riches and power to rule all of the kingdoms of the earth, if Jesus would bow down and worship him. What a coup that would be! Satan must have been drooling with the idea of God worshiping him.

However, Jesus was done. He had fasted forty days, and while his body was weak, his mind and spirit were sharper than ever, and he fought back Satan's best attacks, using the scriptures. Now he is mad and shouts:

Away from me, Satan! For it is written: "Worship the LORD your God, and serve him only" (Deut 6:13).

This brief exchange between Jesus and Satan lasts only eleven verses at the beginning of Matthew chapter 4, but it was deadly serious spiritual warfare—combat. The stakes were staggeringly high—eternal life in heaven for all believers hung in the balance, the fate of those in the dungeon, and the total loss of authority, kingship, and reconciliation for Jesus and the universe.

Satan's ammunition was the ability to misquote God for his own purposes, which we have seen repeatedly in the Bible and in our lives. However, Jesus correctly quoted scripture to push him back.

And it was enough. It was enough for Jesus, and it is enough for us.

As demonstrated by this passage, God's *written* Word has real power. We learn to resist Satan by reading our Bible and quoting the appropriate scriptures when we feel tempted to do wrong: lie, cheat, steal, porn, disobedience, unfaithfulness, drug and alcohol abuse, vengeance, angers, unforgiveness. Many Bibles have a section on Helps with subjects like resisting temptation or finding help in times of need. Some churches do not typically teach on things like spiritual warfare, but you can buy books on the subject.

Then the devil left him, and the angels came and attended him (Matt 4:11).

FASTING

I believe another element of Jesus' power and success lay in the practice of fasting, giving up food. In modern times, people fast from things like television, but we are only interested in giving up food here, the traditional fast. Fasting puts the body in submission to the heart and mind. Fasting is difficult. But it is a spiritual discipline that becomes easier with practice. If you regularly read your Bible, pray often, and attend church regularly, then consider adding this practice as well.

If you have any concerns about your health or medications, please consult a medical professional before fasting.

In Matthew 6:17–18 and 9:15, Jesus talks about fasting as if it is a common practice among believers. Likewise, God explains that the basic goal of fasting (which he assumes we are doing) is to grow powerful in spiritual warfare, but it has obvious benefits also.

Is not this the kind of fasting I (God) have chosen: to loose the chains of injustice and untie the cords of the yoke, to set the oppressed free and break every yoke? Is it not to share your food with the hungry and to provide the poor wanderer with shelter—when you see the naked, to clothe them, and not to turn away from your own flesh and blood? Then your light will break forth like the dawn, and your healing will quickly appear;

then your righteousness will go before you, and the glory of the Lord will be your rear guard (Isa 58:6-8).

Why did I just spend so much time on the spiritual warfare aspect of this engagement? I want to emphasize, again, that *we are at war*, and Jesus is our model for how to fight successfully in it through fasting, prayer, scripture, service, and fellowship.

The Apostle James told us:

Submit yourselves, then, to God. Resist the devil, and he will flee from you (James 4:7).

We submit by obeying what Jesus tells us to do in the Gospels, and by following the teachings of the Apostles. We resist the devil by avoiding those actions that will lead to error in our lives: *"Do not give the devil a foothold"* (Eph 4:27). When we feel attacked—tempted (1 Peter 5:8-9)—quote scripture with authority, which means you have to learn scripture. And remember, the bad thought is just as wrong as the bad action.

Let us take a minute to look at the end of Paul's letter to the Ephesians.

Finally, be strong in the LORD and in his mighty power. Put on the full armor of God, so that you can take your stand against the devil's schemes. For our struggle is not against flesh and blood, but against the rulers, against the authorities, against the powers of this dark world and against the spiritual forces of evil in the heavenly realms. Therefore put on the full armor of God, so that when the day of evil comes, you may be able to stand your ground, and after you have done everything, to stand (Eph 6:10-13).

In this passage, we learn that our fight is not actually against humans, although they may be the ones causing us great grief and sorrow as Satan's agents—often unknowingly. Instead, in your mind, refocus on who the enemy really is, *"the devil's schemes—spiritual forces of evil."* Knowing who the real enemy is allows us to be forgiving of the perpetrator, and it allows us to take the high ground, no longer pathetic victims. Jesus modeled that behavior by forgiving his tormentors from the cross:

"Father, forgive them, for they do not know what they are doing" (Luke 23:34).

Paul tells us that, as soldiers in this conflict, we have a suit of armor at our disposal. I was a soldier, who wore armor. I can tell you that we had to know how to wear it, how to use it, and how to care for it. Experienced soldiers train in their armor, wear the armor with confidence, and use it effectively when fighting the enemy.

Stand firm then, with the belt of truth buckled around your waist, with the breastplate of righteousness in place, and with your feet fitted with the readiness that comes from the gospel of peace. In addition to all this, take up the shield of faith, with which you can extinguish all the flaming arrows of the evil one. Take the helmet of salvation and the sword of the Spirit, which is the Word of God (Eph 6:14-17).

Roman soldier in full armor.

Some of these pieces sound metaphorical: *"a belt of truth—a breastplate of righteousness."* But a flaming arrow is anything "shot" at you that makes you wince in pain—the words and actions of others—coming at you from the outside, or words and actions against yourself—coming at you from the inside, by Satan's promptings and revealed as self-abuse, judgment, and criticism.

All of this armor is defensive until we get to the Sword of the Spirit—the Word of God—the Bible. Jesus used it as an offensive weapon when tempted, and so can you. Become proficient with this weapon. Use it professionally and wisely, and you will be victorious when Satan or his minions attack, directly or by using your fellow human beings.

Memorize this verse and quote it every time you are tempted to do something you know is wrong:

No temptation has overtaken me except what is common to everyone. God is faithful; he will not let me be tempted beyond what I can bear. But when I am tempted, he will also provide a way out so that I can endure it (1 Cor 10:13, personalized).

This is a promise of God you can stand firm on. Memorize other scriptures you might need so your sword is powerful and effective. As with any weapons training, especially sword work, you only get better with lots of practice.

THE

CHAPTER FOURTEEN

ANCIENT ONES

Apparently, the Garden of Eden was on Earth, but not necessarily in our physical universe. How could it be? Obviously, if the Garden were in our physical universe, we would still see it or be aware of that peculiar plot of land denied to us. Instead, God expelled Adam and Eve, and an angel was set to guard the Tree of Life, so they and their new children did not eat of it and live forever. But not on the physical Earth we occupy.

After he drove the man out, he placed on the east side of the Garden of Eden cherubim and a flaming sword flashing back and forth to guard the way to the tree of life (Gen 3:24).

Let me stop here for a second.

After God expelled Adam and Eve, why did he place an angel on guard duty? To stop Adam and his children born *after* the Fall from eating the Tree of Life fruit, and thus living forever in sin under the curse. That means it must be possible for people, either on purpose or by accident, to get back into the Garden where the tree lives. Otherwise, a guard would not be necessary.

So why don't we see this enclave between two rivers—perhaps somewhere in the Middle East or Africa? Is it all Biblical mythology? Did a great flood or movement of the continents destroy the Garden?

If you could travel into the spiritual world, you would still see a cherubim angel standing at the trailhead on the path to the Tree of Life with a flaming sword flashing back and forth. So I believe it still exists *in the other dimension*—the spiritual dimension. What evidence leads to this conclusion?

For that answer, let us go back to the beginning.

God created everything and made people to supervise creation. He gave Adam the task of naming the animals (Gen 2:19-20). We read that Adam was busy about this work for some time. We don't know how long; it could have been a long, long time. Later on, he desired a mate. God provided Eve. They lived happily in the Garden and life was simple and uncomplicated.

The Garden was *Perfect* with a capital *P*. Ideal. Made for them in every way. No cares. No needs. No worries. No illness. No fighting. All the basic needs satisfied and easily gathered foods. They could fashion simple shelters from the rain. Makes me think of some Amazonian tribes, living in harmony with the jungle. The temperature range was tolerable since they had no clothes. Innocent. Gentle. Humble. The Bible says God had the habit of walking through Eden in the cool of the day and I can imagine Adam joining him—I would (Gen 3:8). How amazing is that? I do not believe anyone in their right mind would want to mess up a life this beautiful.

It appears that Adam and his family had the ability to leave the safety of the Garden, venturing into the physical world, coming and going. Exploring. The Garden in the spiritual realm was safe; the physical world not so much.

How long did this go on?

How long were Adam and Eve in the Garden—in this perfect environment under God's watchful and loving eye?

Adam and Eve are Driven Out of Eden by Paul Gustave Doré (1832–1883).

You can read the first three chapters of Genesis in a few minutes; creation and the events that follow move right along. One minute God creates Adam and Eve and they are enjoying life; the next minute they mess things up and are out on their ears. Did it happen that quickly?

No. Not at all.

I believe Adam was in the Garden a long time by himself, and then Adam and Eve were in the Garden a long, long time together, before what we call the Fall.

How long?

Would it shock you to imagine them living in this unspoiled amazing paradise for 400 million years?

Yes—you are shocked.

Four hundred million is a big number, however used. Did I mention that I have rock-solid evidence of this?

Why do I say 400 million years? Why this criteria?

In 1844, in the Kingoodie Quarry of Northern England, Sir David Brewster discovered a nail firmly embedded in a block of sandstone—unseen until the sandstone was broken open. That sandstone strata has been dated to 360 to 480 million years old.

In 1912, Frank Kennard, while working at a coal plant, found a piece too large to use, so he broke it in half with a sledge hammer. Out fell an iron pot. He traced the piece of coal to the Wilburton, Oklahoma, coal mines. That layer of coal was created during the Mesozoic Era—300 million years old by geological standards—from the age of the dinosaurs when a single continent called Pangaea existed. No ice caps at the poles and balmy warm weather throughout. The Mesozoic Era includes the Triassic, the Jurassic we are all familiar with from the movies, and the Cretaceous.

In 1944, Newton Anderson of West Virginia dropped a lump of coal, which split open revealing a brass bell. He had the bell analyzed at the University of Oklahoma. It contained known metals but in an unusual blend, also 300 million years old.

Fossilized trilobite approximately 252–521 million years old. *Credit: www.publicdomainpictures.net/.*

In June 1968, William J. Meister, hunting for fossils with his wife and two daughters at Antelope Springs near Delta, Utah, split open a slab of rock with his rock hammer and discovered inside a fossilized human footprint, wearing a sandal—approximately ten inches by three inches—that had also stepped on a trilobite. This layer of shale is from 280 to 320 million years old.

A month later, in July 1968, Dr. Clifford Burdick, a Tucson, Arizona, geologist found a fossilized child's footprint in the shale deposits in the

Antelope Springs area. He noted that the impression in the mud indicated toes spreading, like that of a child who never wore shoes.

In 1981, in a coal vein near Mahanoy, Pennsylvania, Ed Conrad found a petrified human skull in a coal deposit, tentatively dated at 280 million years.

TIMING AND DATING

Some people do not trust radioactive Carbon 14 (C-14) dating. Scientists and Creationists go back and forth in this area. Some Creationists start with the premise that the earth is actually young. They say that the Bible clearly says the earth is less than 10,000 years old (although some admit, perhaps up to 100,000 years old), which automatically puts them at odds with C-14 dating. The problem is that the Creationists start with a false assumption that Adam and Eve failed shortly after their creation. This cannot be known, because the Bible is only concerned with the account of humans and life in general on this planet *after the Fall*, not before.

How long is God's day?

What is a day to God? Is it twenty-four hours? Is the creation account based on something we don't fully understand about God's timing, methods, and purposes? Even if we take the Bible literally—Earth created in six standard twenty-four-hour days—that also does not limit how long Adam and Eve were in the Garden. Should we date some coal deposits at 250 million years or 40,000 years? Should the total time allotted for the earth's creation be 100,000 years instead of 4.5 billion? Perhaps we need another method of dating to know for sure.

That brings me to another issue—the speed of light. Astronomers and physicists can clearly determine that stars and shining objects are millions of light years away, so they measure the age of the universe in billions of years. Between the creation of Light and Darkness in Genesis 1:3–5 and the creation of the Sun and Moon in verses 14–19, a great span of time must have elapsed.

Also between Genesis 1:3–5 and verse 14, the sun and moon are not there, so the concept of earth rotation in relation to the sun is nonexistent. In other words, the twenty-four-hour day does not exist yet.

Then what is a day when a day does not exist?

It is whatever God wants it to be. He could still say he created everything in six days and rested the seventh, commanding us to do the same (Exodus 20:8-11).

How can that be?

This is important: *Because God has the ability to move laterally through time.* He can create the stars in one day (however he measures it), and then simply move to what he calls the beginning of the next day or phase to start the following creation event. To God, six creation events take place on six sequential and separate "days," although in the cosmic scheme of things, many millions and billions of years pass between some of them.

The book of Job is supposed to be the oldest book in the Bible. What animal is God describing in Job 40:15–24?

Look at the Behemoth, which I made along with you and which feeds on grass like an ox. What strength it has in its loins, what power in the muscles of its belly!

At this point, we could stop and imagine an elephant or hippopotamus. However, when the description continues, we discover that there is no living creature like it on the earth—now. *"Its tail sways like a cedar; the sinews of its thighs are close knit. Its bones are tubes of bronze, its limbs like rods of iron."*

Tail sways like a cedar. Only the family of dinosaurs known as sauropods (brachiosaurus, brontosaurus, apatosaurus, etc.) accurately fit this description. Created *"along with you."* Four hundred million years ago.

There are many more examples, but let me stop here for a second. The Bible tells us God created life on earth—that there was a specific moment when he did certain things.

Genesis 1:20 says God created the creatures of the oceans and birds before he created the animals on the land.

And God said, "Let the land produce living creatures according to their kinds: livestock, (animals prone to domestication—sheep, cattle, goats) *creatures that move along the ground, and wild animals, each according to its kind."And it was so* (Gen 1:24).

When I read that scientists describe a sudden *and unexpected* creation event in the rocks, approximately 530 million years ago, commonly known as the Cambrian Explosion, I am not surprised. The Bible already describes it.

What is a theory?

A theory is a proposed explanation based on conjecture. We should call some theories maxims or truths. The theory of relativity is one of those proven to be accurate and true early on. But the theory of evolution has always been more of an assumption or argument.

The theory of evolution is based upon the opinion that no other *natural explanation* for creation exists. But when evolutionary scientists say there is no other "natural explanation," they mean their theory has scientific merit based on empirical evidence and is, therefore, believable—even if flawed, while the written biblical and historical account does not, falling perhaps under the categories of myth or fable, because it is a *supernatural explanation* (anything God does is basically supernatural). Their verifiable evidence is in the geological story—easily seen in the rocks, with observable differences in strata, plants, and creatures, measured with scientific instruments.

That argument further presupposes that the scientific theory of an event, like creation, is of more value than an ancient story passed down to us by the alien beings responsible for the creation event itself. The Bible tells us that one of the alien beings inspired humans to write down the creation story and others, to ensure we understood what happened and why it was important.

Above all, you must understand that NO prophecy of Scripture (Biblical stories, books, and letters) *came about by the prophet's own interpretation* (imagination). *For prophecy never had its origin in the will of man, but men spoke from God as they were carried along by the Holy Spirit"* (2 Peter 1:20-21).

The aliens or angels did not hand us a book (well, God did give Moses the Ten Commandments, which he broke shortly after in a fit of rage—Exodus 32:19). Instead, they inspired people to write down the accounts so we would have the knowledge of what happened and how the earliest events fit into our world view and understanding of ourselves in relation to a Creator.

Humans probably passed down the stories of creation in an oral tradition. Adam could say, "There I was . . ." But at different points in time, the Holy Spirit, part of the Triune God—the original alien(s), inspired people to write down what happened in such a way that, despite so many authors, there is a flow of continuity, style, and purpose in our Bible: the story of the human race from beginning to end. Our Bible—Old and New Testaments— is not something humans constructed, but was given to us by God; therefore, we cannot arbitrarily change it to fit our evolving social or cultural ideas and thinking.

I want you to know, brothers and sisters, that the gospel I preached is not of human origin. I did not receive it from any man, nor was I taught it; rather, I received it by revelation from Jesus Christ (Gal 1:11-12).

People cannot accuse early Christians of tampering with the book of Genesis, because we have copies from before the time of Jesus. Genesis records ten generations from Adam to the Flood, who are ancestors in the line leading to Jesus Christ (Genesis 5). Adam means *Man*. The name of his son, Seth, means *Appointed*. His grandson, Enosh, means *Mortal Sickness*. Kenan came next and his name means *Sorrow*. Mahalalel means *The Blessed of God*. Jared means *Shall Come Down*. Enoch means *Teaching*. Methusaleh, who lived longer than anyone outside the Garden, means *his Death Shall Bring*. Lamech means *Despairing*, and Noah means *Comfort*.

When we write out the name meanings, they look like this: *Man is appointed mortal sickness and sorrow, but the Blessed of God shall come down teaching that his death shall bring the despairing comfort.*

Interesting. We discover God's plan of redemption through the genealogy of Jesus Christ at the beginning of Genesis. What a coincidence.

Here is a big one.

Why is the Cambrian Explosion event unexpected by archeologists, paleontologists, and evolutionists? Because there is no "lead up" in the fossil record as predicted by the theory of evolution.

By lead up, I mean small creatures that would become large, those without legs that would crawl out of the water and walk on land, water breathers who become air breathers, flightless creatures that would become flying creatures later: no time of transitional change. What we find is an explosion of life in all of its diversity, dependencies, mimicry, symbiotic relationships, and wonder.

This also means, I believe, that every variation of creatures existed at one time, *at the same time*. For example, we have fish (water breathers only), then we have fish that breathe water and air (tetrapods, lungfish, certain catfish and eels, the snakehead), and fish that breathe air and walk on land (amphibious fish like the mudskipper). This is not evolution, it is diversity, observable to this day.

Just because someone digs up a small hominid creature in Africa (hominid: creatures that walk upright on two legs, bipedal, from extinct to modern, including humans, apes, monkeys), does not automatically mean it is a human ancestor. It just means another creature similar to us existed at the same time—as they do now. However, if your belief or hope is in evolution—the non-God alternative—the biased thinking and outcomes will reflect that.

In November 1974, in Hadar, Ethiopia, palaeontologist Donald Johanson discovered the bones later described as Lucy—the size and shape of a chimpanzee. Her bones were dated at approximately 3.2 million years old, and yet Dr. Johanson believed she was a possible early ancestor. Dr. Johanson said, "Lucy was not [human]. No matter what kind of clothes were put on Lucy, she would not look like a human being. She was too far back, out of the human range entirely. On the hominid line the earliest ones are too primitive to be called humans. They must be given another name. Lucy is in that category."[1]

Lucy is not human at all. But some scientists have assumed that she is a missing link between the most ancient hominids and us. Not a chance. Humans, as we know them, were already here, so how could Lucy be an ancestor? Lucy is just another relative of the chimpanzee family she so closely resembles.

Even Charles Darwin marveled at the sudden diversification of the Cambrian Explosion. He pondered, "To the question why we do not find rich fossiliferous deposits belonging to these assumed earliest periods prior to the Cambrian system, I can give no satisfactory answer."[2]

"—assumed earliest periods."

Why is this statement from Darwin important? Because as Darwin worked out the theory of evolution, even he had doubts. Without a satisfactory interpretation, we must admit that the Bible has presented the only plausible explanation for what occurred.

Scientists say the Cambrian Explosion produced the mass diversification of life we know today with complex organisms in their peculiar ecological niches, symbiotic relationships, dependencies, and competitions. But what I find extremely interesting is that it was all in equilibrium—balanced—in harmony.

The Cambrian Explosion arrived with intact symbiotic relationships that benefit either species, or only one of the two involved. This is an indication of the elaborate complexity and intricacy, and evidence of an active hand in that involvement. I mean, what other proof does a scientist need? Here is the evidence itself, which causes them to scratch their heads in consternation.

There are different kinds of symbiotic relations: Mutualistic—two different species benefit from the relationship, cooperating for mutual success. Some flowers depend on bats and insects for pollination. Gut flora allow humans to more efficiently digest food and apparently affect us in other ways.

Commensalism is from the Latin for *sharing a table*: One organism enjoying the relationship at the expense of another, who gains nothing through the sharing of food, shelter, or transportation. The buzzard waits for the wolf to finish eating. Pilot fish and remoras do the same, eating scraps left behind by larger fish and sharks. Cow waste in the field applies much needed fertilizer to the grasses and plants they eat. Crocodiles serviced by plovers, rainforest caterpillars and leaf hoppers feeding ants and being protected by them, zebras in cooperation with oxpeckers and ostriches, cleaner shrimp and gobys eating parasites on large fish, sea anemones housing clown fish, honeyguide birds working with ratels and honey badgers and even humans. Go to the Internet and type in "amazing symbiotic relationships" and be amazed.

Nile crocodile and Egyptian plover.

What happened to the first plover that ventured into the crocodile's mouth in search of food bits? Croc breakfast? Not at all! From the very beginning, God created the plover to enter boldly and fearlessly into the tooth-filled jaws, at the same time giving the croc the idea of this bird helping. Mutual benefit.

Parasitic—one species takes advantage of another, who may even suffer in the relationship. Almost all animals have parasites. The tick, flea, and mosquito suck blood and some transfer diseases to the host. Have you seen programs on television where the tarantula wasp lays eggs in the big spider, that then hatch with a ready meal at hand? Viruses, bacteria, and protozoa fit easily into this category. In some instances, the host sickens and dies (parasitoid). But mostly, we tolerate the relationship, however annoying it may be.

Monarch butterfly.

We visited Pacific Grove, California, to see the bright orange and black butterflies flying through the eucalyptus trees. Biologists marvel at the 1,500-mile migration of these marvelous insects—to and from Mexico, wondering how they started this great feat, how routes were determined, and why they continue this ritual over the years. Amazingly, young monarchs do not learn from older monarchs, because a generation is lost: It takes three generations to make the round trip.

Who determined that the monarch butterflies would not mature fully as the days shortened, instead storing up energy for the great trip ahead? How is the memory of the migration transmitted to those yet to be born? The scientist asks "what and how?" while we know the "who" but also ask "what and how?" Even though we assume the *who,* we can still dive into the mechanics of the *how.* And we should.

Is not this another fingerprint of God?—a sign of someone actively at work in creation from the molecular and microscopic level to the enormous and macroscopic?

Four things are small, yet they are extremely wise. Ants are creatures of little strength, yet they store up food in the summer. Locusts have no king, yet they advance together in ranks (Proverb 30:24-25, 27).

The peculiarities, eccentricities, quirks, and nuances of animal and insect behavior (including some plants and trees) are the stuff of documentaries that amaze and delight us. I watched a PBS program on animal and insect mimicry and thought how only God could have set that up. I never get tired of watching *March of the Penguins* or *Nature* on PBS. As a kid, I spent hours and hours watching ants turn a blue-belly fence lizard into an exquisite skeleton.

Solomon understood something:

It is the glory of God to conceal a matter; to search out the matter is the glory of kings. (kings or wise and learned people—Proverbs 25:2).

I was struck by an article about the myxozoa (*mik-so-zoa*); a peculiar parasite of only twelve cells, related to the jellyfish and corals. The author started the article by saying, "We typically think of evolution as a progression from simplicity to complexity. But one organism seems to have thrown the rulebook out the window—"[3]

This is what I am saying: that the Cambrian Explosion resulted in all creatures settled in their niche modes, perfectly adapted, perfectly in harmony, from simple to complex.

What came first: the chicken or the egg?

Think about it: What came first, the chicken or the egg? The chicken! At the moment of creation, there were enough chickens to sustain themselves biologically—male and female, create eggs with chicks to prolong their existence, the inclination and proclivity to nurture their offspring, and plenty of the little critters to provide food for those animals able to catch them. So it was with all creatures, from the mightiest earth walkers and swimmers, to grasses, plants, and trees, down to the smallest bacteria and viruses: all of the complexity and entanglement of life in balance and harmony, including symbiosis, keystone hierarchies, mimicry, and camouflage. Suddenly and wonderfully.

Yes, when God was finished, he was well pleased. And ready to take a break. Not because he was tired—that is impossible. But because he was perfectly D O N E and pleased with the final result.

What we find in the geological and paleontological record is a complete and sudden diversification, not a slow transformation of evolving systems of life as theorized by Darwin. In other words, God created the starfish with its simple eyes that can barely distinguish between light and dark at the same time he created the octopus with its complex and sophisticated eye. Even Darwin wondered if he was getting that analogy right, when he suggested that a simple eye evolved into a complex eye.

> To suppose that the eye with all its inimitable contrivances for adjusting the focus to different distances, for admitting different amounts of light, and for the correction of spherical and chromatic aberration, could have been formed by natural selection, seems, I freely confess, absurd in the highest degree.[4]

Charles Darwin, 1809–1882. *Photograph by John G. Murdoch 1874.*

Having written this confession—another version of his nagging doubts—he quickly turned around and said he still believed in the idea of evolving organs.

On another note, Darwin wrote, "The mystery of the beginning of all things is insoluble by us; and I for one must be content to remain an agnostic."[5]

Of course, I disagree with this statement. The "mystery of the beginning of all things" is not insoluble if we are willing to approach the study with an open mind and equally open heart. Darwin called himself an agnostic, a new term at the time.

An agnostic is someone who believes in God (or a god), but is opposed to the extremes of unbridled faith on one side and faithlessness on the other, or is unwilling to just take any such belief by faith. I know scientists who simply will not believe in God, because it is not "scientific." And many more because their real problem is with the Church.

PROOF OF GOD

But what of the person who professes faith in God, yet loves the scientific, rational, and empirical search for knowledge? Are the two incompatible? Not unless you want them to be. Didn't the quotes from Einstein speak of this possibility? The scientist asks, "How do I exist?" The philosopher asks, "Why do I exist?" Theologically, I believe God wants us to study and explore all avenues and possibilities without denying him, searching for him in all disciplines and details: to seek out what he has deliberately concealed. I imagine God nodding approvingly and smiling when we discover something like gluons.

However, to me the question moves into theological existentialism, why we exist rests alongside how we exist, because the "why" addresses our behavior and speaks to transcendent purpose and an existence after our lives here end—death and resurrection. I am here, then what? And, so what?

I understand the scientist's predicament. As stated earlier, the scientist wants empirical evidence. Science is a search for truth, but is the result discounted or invalid if it points to a supernatural conclusion? Or suggests a Creator? A lot of what I am trying to do in this book is appeal to either overt or covert evidence of alien involvement in our creation story. An alien we can discover—and know.

More than physical creation came out of the Cambrian Explosion. Along with created things, we experience virtues: intangibles like goodness, morality, integrity, love, courage, dignity, worthiness, nobility, and honor. Not just life: we also see purpose and meaning. Not just the hand of God: we see the deep grooves of the fingerprint leading to the finger, the finger to the hand, the hand to the owner. Our alien.

Can you be a follower of Christ and still believe the theory of evolution adequately addresses the origin of all species on Earth? I think I have shown that there are holes in that idea, clues in the geological record readily seen and understood (human footprints with dinosaurs prints), and the main purpose of the evolutionary theory might be to suggest that a Greater Hand was *not* involved.

Still, I have met people who choose to believe the theory of evolution, no matter what evidence shows otherwise, and most of them are not even scientists. Why? It is easier to believe in something "scientific," even if based wholly on conjecture and absurdity, than proclaim a simple faith in God, the Author of this life explosion, who cannot be strictly verified in a laboratory—which I think he prefers.

A friend of mine believes that God used evolution to create life on Earth. When I described the Cambrian Explosion, he replied that the whole Genesis account was a myth and unbelievable. The problem with this thinking is that you cannot cherry-pick the Bible. The Bible is an all or nothing proposition; you cannot pick and choose what you will believe or not believe. An acquaintance said, "Jesus never said he was the Son of God." I was astonished: "What? He says it over and over in the Gospel of John." He replied, "Well, I don't believe or accept the Gospel of John." How convenient: If you do not agree with it, you do not accept it.

If you do not agree with something in the Bible, or you wonder about what is going on or happening in a passage, that does not mean it is false until proven true. And you cannot reject those parts that make you uncomfortable or don't fit your worldview and perspective.

Legally, I would say there is overwhelming circumstantial evidence. I know Christian people who believe the theory of evolution addresses all creation. When I suggest that God created all things, as explained in the Bible and through geological evidence, they roll their eyes. Oh well. I guess I am provincial and unenlightened.

I find evidence for knowledge of God through the Bible *and in science*—one informs the other. My bias is obvious, but I believe it is an honest bias, because both the Bible and science reveal our alien through our search for how systems work in *his universe*.

Gluons are a good example, as mentioned earlier. I mean, if God created everything, then science would be a quest to discover his fingerprints on practically everything. Actually, some scientists might prefer to say they find the fingerprints of *aliens* on some things. Is that stubbornness?

Another friend told me there was no conclusive proof of God, but isn't the Cambrian Explosion a type of proof? My friend, a computer scientist, is an affirmed atheist, who denies the existence of God, but even he admits that he takes his denial on blind faith. For him rationalism serves as his belief system. (He would not want me to use the word religion.) I like this quote from Werner Heisenberg, the Father of Quantum Physics:

> The first gulp from the glass of natural sciences will turn you into an atheist, but at the bottom of the glass God is waiting for you.[6]

Is it possible that as these learned men plumb the depths of how the universe works, they begin to see the shadow of God, hazy at first, but growing clearer and more obvious the more they learn? If true, then the atheist, at least those who appeal to science and rationalism for their disbelief, is revealed in stubborn denial. Perhaps they should re-examine their disbelief system, ponder what Einstein and others fellow scientists discovered, and shore it up with some other idea or theory.

ADAPTATION

The problem with the idea of Natural Selection is it begs the question: Who does the selection? Environmental stress is the common answer, although that does not empirically explain whom or what does the selection. Over the centuries, many creatures have gone extinct because of local and global disasters (think Noah's flood), changes in the geology, climate, atmosphere, environment, and hunters. Some creatures adapt better compared to others, surviving these changes. This is not an endorsement of evolution, but rather an anticipated response to changes built into the system, programmed into the DNA of all creatures.

But I have always been bothered by the geology. If all animals were here at one time, wouldn't we find lion or elephant bones among tyrannosaurus rex bones? If there was one land mass, Pangea, did great rivers, seas, and plateaus separate some or most of the species? Were great inland seas the home of fierce aquatic species, while benign creatures lived in other areas?

Technically, we find many dinosaurs in hardened mud. They either lived in swamps and seashores or were swept into mud and sand deposits by floods or catastrophes. Different animals lived in different regions. Even today, Africa and Australia host a variety of plants and animals not found on other continents. Did various landmasses and seas provide the ideal environment for certain creatures and not others?

The answer to these questions is that, on occasion, paleontologists do find mammals among the dinosaur bones, but the findings are not emphasized. "And the Institute for Creation Research's front lobby features a juvenile hadrosaur taken from the Two Medicine Formation—a sandstone formation which extends from the east side of the Rocky Mountains eastward to Edmonton, Canada—that was fossilized alongside marine clams and snails, as well as birds, mammals, and other dinosaurs."[7]

Dr. Don Batten said:

Few [people] are aware of the great number of mammal species found with dinosaurs. Paleontologists have found 432 mammal species in the dinosaur layers; almost as many as the number of dinosaur species. These include nearly 100 complete mammal skeletons. But where are these fossils? We visited 60 museums but did not see a single complete mammal skeleton from the dinosaur layers displayed at any of these museums. This is amazing. Also, we saw only a few dozen incomplete skeletons/single bones of the 432 mammal species found so far. Why don't the museums display these mammal fossils and also the bird fossils?"[8]

Some creatures could not tolerate a colder climate, and died off, while others preferred a cooler climate and thrived. Changes in atmospheric composition or ocean salinity might kill off one creature while another does not notice the change, and still another thrives better than before. When an asteroid struck and made life unbearable on the earth, it seems that many smaller animals prospered while larger creatures suffered—on land and in the oceans. The fact that every possible configuration of animal once lived on the earth, ensured that many would adapt and flourish whatever happened. Some survive, some die off.

Scientists call the nautilus a living fossil—ancient and modern, because they find the nautilus in deposits dating back 400 to 500 million years, while scientists admit they have not evolved much since—*if at all.* Crocodiles have been around 200 million years by some accounts. The coelacanth fish was supposed to have gone extinct 65 to 80 million years ago, with some fossils dated at 360 million years. But in 1938, a living coelacanth was caught by fishermen in the western Indian Ocean. So it has been around all along. A recent *Discovery* channel documentary seems to show evidence of a megalodon great shark, living at great depths, which is also supposed to be extinct. It seems creatures have the ability to adapt, surviving despite extreme changes. In Thailand, a small blind fish can walk on land. Does that automatically mean that this two-inch cavefish explains how creatures evolved in the seas and then walked on land? Not at all. God made the Cryptotora thamicola to do this from the beginning.

While stationed with the US Army at Fort Irwin, California, in the Mojave Desert—30 miles north of Barstow—we adapted to the extremely hot temperatures. On 3 July 1984, up on a ridge known as Red Lake Pass, our thermometer read 137 degrees Fahrenheit (58.33 Celsius). Down in the valley by The Whale—a basalt peninsula of rocks—the same thermometer read 146 (63.3 C). The desert floor was 165 (73.8 C). Hot. Yet, we walked around with dark-colored, long-sleeved shirts. At sunset, the temperature quickly dropped to 90 degrees (32.2 C) and we felt cold—a 40 to 50 degree drop in a few minutes. I had to wrap myself up in the army green wool blanket to stay warm.

How did this work?

A doctor told me that, over time, our bodies adapted to the hot weather by thinning the blood to aide in cooling. We, and apparently all creatures, including plants and trees, have the ability to adapt—to a point—to the extreme changes in climate. If not able to adapt effectively, many creatures migrate to find an ecological niche that better suits their needs.

For our survival, the continuous and personal changes in complexity and diversity that all living things experience in order to survive, seems to be crafted into our DNA. Another fingerprint.

Albert Einstein said it this way:

The scientists' religious feeling takes the form of a rapturous amazement at the *harmony* of natural law, which reveals an intelligence of such superiority that, compared with it, all the systematic thinking and acting of human beings is an utterly insignificant reflection (italics mine).[9]

Smart man that Albert, who reached the pinnacle of rational and scientific thought, yet remained humble enough to realize it was a gift of God; that through physics, he was really searching for God's fingerprints on the universe.

He also said:

I want to know how God created this world. I am not interested in this or that phenomenon, in the spectrum of this or that element. I want to know his thoughts; the rest are details.[10]

I feel the same way.

Four hundred million years—old.

While I have been careful to not report findings that are overtly controversial, there are many more stories of unusual items found in 400-plus-million-year-old coal and shale deposits, and equally amazing items have been found in the rock and sediment dating from 400 million years into the more recent past.

The list of discoveries like this goes on and on, most of which are authenticated but leave us scratching our heads. It is not surprising that, along with the many books on the subject, there are equally as many skeptics. And of course, talk of aliens.

Some people are skeptical simply because humans were not supposed to be around during the time of the dinosaurs, whatever the evidence. How can they refute footprints only discovered when someone split open the shale for the first time since the mud was stepped in so many millions of years ago? It might be that some era charts will need to be updated. They certainly need to stop saying, "This pre-dates humans . . ."

Some do not believe the Adam and Eve story (seeing the Bible as just a history book), so they do not care about any of this and would rather talk about alien visitors. Then there are people who are skeptical because they believe Adam and Eve were only in the Garden a relatively short time before the Fall—a few years at most. Finally, some people believe all conjecture like this is wrong.

The first group will call the 400-million-year idea flawed and wish I had talked more about aliens, or Ezekiel's wheeled flying machine. The second group will not buy any of this and probably do not really care. The third group will barely get through a book like this and call it heretical. Well, skeptics are always critical of new ideas. I am just glad we do not burn different-thinking people at the stake anymore.

ALIEN

CHAPTER FIFTEEN

RELATIVES

NEANDERTHAL

Through the evidence of more than 400 bones, scientists believe proto-Neanderthal humans lived in Eurasia between 350,000 and 600,000 years ago. They had larger brains and human DNA—not human-like, but human. Then they believe "true Neanderthals" lived up to 300,000 years ago, or more. Below are images of Neanderthals based on skeleton reconstruction.

Sculpture of Neanderthal man with modern girl. *Credit: Kennis&Kennis/NeanderthalMuseum.*

Neanderthal sculpture.

I have news for you; I have seen many people who look like this. Indo-European races, some Middle Eastern peoples, and various tribes of Native Americans have the sloping forehead, large nose, and high cheekbones. It might be that the Neanderthal people actually lived all over the world, although most evidence is from bones found in southern Europe extending over to the Middle East and Asia. We might be seeing hints of their presence among us. Scientists believe the Neanderthal people were absorbed into our race, and the pictures above support that conclusion.

I bring this up because I believe Adam and Eve lived in the Garden of Eden an exceptionally long time—had many kids, who then had many kids, and so on.

When Adam and Eve ate of the forbidden fruit, God said to Eve, "*I will greatly increase your pains in childbearing; with pain you will give birth to children*" (Gen 3:16). In other words, from now on when you have kids, it will be strikingly painful. Conclusion: She must have had kids *without pain*. Otherwise, what difference would this punishment make?

What does this mean? It means that when God expelled Adam and Eve from the Garden, *they were not alone.*

I am sure many people had been leaving the Garden for thousands of years (hence the Neanderthal bones) venturing into our world to explore and live their lives. Why would they leave the Garden paradise? Three possible answers: Perhaps the Garden became over-populated. Some may have wanted to live and explore outside the Garden. And then a few may have been expelled for eating of the Tree of Knowledge. The people who left the Garden voluntarily had the ability to move freely between the spiritual Garden and our physical Earth.

And they still can.

Because the Garden of Eden still exists, is full of people, and some of them are quite advanced—*now, today.*

ALIENS AMONG US

We have already talked about how Adam and Eve could have been in the Garden for millions of years. God ejected these two people for their disobedience, *but not their children.* The immortals living there do not experience death, disease, addictions, mental illness, nothing that would bring about our typical modern day pains, aches, sorrows—and death. They would be regularly and dynamically healthy, *and immortal.*

This idea would solve some long-standing mysteries.

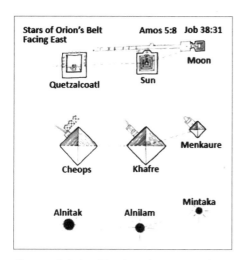

Alignment similarity of Egyptian and Mayan pyramids and stars of Orion's belt. *Credit drawing: "Mystery of the Crystal Skulls" Ceri Thomas and Chris Morton.*

Carbon 14 analysis of wood and plant material in the mortar of some pyramids date them to around 2690 BC. But some people believe the three great pyramids of Giza, along with the Sphinx, were constructed closer to 10,500 BC, based on their alignment to the stars. A small group suggests the pyramids might be much older, perhaps more than 20,000 years—before people were supposed to be around and able to complete such a monumental task. However, there are clues that might make them much older.

The Teotihuacan pyramids of Mexico were constructed in the same pattern as the three pyramids in Giza—aligned the same way, with the center pyramid exactly half the size of the second pyramid in Egypt. How is that possible? One story tells how the Mayan peoples migrated into Central America *and found the pyramids already there.* Another story suggests that these pyramids are at least 20,000 years old.

Who built these pyramids and why? And although 7,000 miles apart—across a great ocean—similar in layout?

Could it be that the three pyramids laid out like the stars in Orion's belt are trying to tell us about other civilizations? Some have shown how the Sphinx—a great resting lion—points to the constellation of Leo the Lion.

Lion superimposed over Sphinx.

Originally, the Sphinx had the head of a lion. If it were actually ancient, that would explain why weather heavily eroded the body. It would have been worse, but for many years, sand covered most of the body, protecting it from erosion. Apparently, at one time, something damaged the head, so a pharaoh had it sculpted into his likeness, which explains why the head seems much too small for the rest of the sculpture.

Sphinx covered in sand.

Two of the brightest stars in the constellation of Leo the Lion are Regulus and Denebola. Perhaps a civilization of lion-like creatures live in either the solar system of Regulus, Little King, 77.5 light years away, or Denebola, The Lion's Tale, 36 light years away, or both. In the constellation of Leo, there is a sun similar to ours, Gliese 436—30 light years away and above Denebola, with a large earth-like planet in orbit.

Someone built the pyramids to last, and they did despite geological changes, so later generations would see and wonder and perhaps discover something in the clues: that we might be part of a bigger picture, part of a cosmic story.

I believe our relatives in the Garden created the three great pyramids of Giza. They had the ability to talk to God and learn about life on other planets, and they had the technology and time to build structures that would last.

Have you heard of the Bimini Road? Fifty-eight miles due east of Miami, off the coast of North Bimini Island in the Bahamas in eighteen feet (5.5 meters) of water, is what appears to be a half-mile-long road or wall (based on what we can see—there may be more) made from stone blocks with an average span of ten feet. Natural or man-made? Some have compared these blocks to the pyramids in Giza in size and shape, and there might be another layer underneath. If these stones were set on dry land, then someone built the road or wall during the Sangamonian interglacial stage between 75,000 and 125,000 years ago.

Is there a connection? Could the pyramids in Giza be as old as this wall—built 100,000 years ago, then appropriated by the pharaohs for their own use when the Egyptians moved into the Nile delta area? Something else to ponder.

The ocean remains a mystery. The legend of Atlantis, sunken cities, strange underwater objects, and treasure ships pique our interest and make us wonder what else might be going on down there, and how long ago. Old maps cause excitement because they seem to pull navigational and land mass information from ancient source material—much older maps. The margin notes of the Piri Reis map, from 1513, tells readers that he used information from Portuguese sailors blown off course during a storm. However, different people have shown how a portion of the Antarctic continent on the map might be from *before* ice covered everything.

The Oronteus Finaeus map of 1531, Carte des Terres Australes, using known and *unknown* ancient sources, accurately depicts rivers, bays, and estuaries, *and no ice on the Ross Sea*, where a great ice shelf now sits, 1,000 to 2,300 feet (300 to 700 meters) thick. The ice cap on Antarctica is supposed to be more than one million years old, although there have been periods of minor melting.

So who made these maps? And when could they have been made, showing an ice-free Antarctic continent?

Antarctica was warm and tropical 46 to 53 million years ago—completely ice free. The journal *Nature* published the results of Antarctic drilling off Wilkes Land by the Integrated Ocean Drilling Program, showing that the continent was once warm and high in carbon dioxide, soil bacteria, fossilized spores, and pollen. This led researches to determine that sub-tropical and tropical rainforests with southern beech and Araucaria trees covered the coasts of the continent.

"It was a green beautiful place," said Professor Jane Francis, of Leeds University's School of Earth and Environment. "Lots of furry mammals, including possums and beavers lived there. The weather was tropical. It is only in the recent geological past that it got so cold."[1]

I wonder how many of these ancient maps have been found but written off as hoaxes, because people were not supposed to be wandering around back then, much less creating maps of their travels.

"Anasazi" means *Ancient Strangers.* Their Navajo neighbors thought they were from *another place.* In the 1200's AD, they simply disappeared. Did the Anasazi see the migration of violent tribes into their territory and decide to return to the Garden where it was safer?

I am suggesting that before and after the Fall, the children of Adam and Eve, who continued in the Garden and remained immortal, made maps to share with others about what they'd discovered as they sailed the seas and explored our world. They watched the continents slowly drift apart. They found places where they wanted to build something lasting as a way of helping us learn about the universe.

The three great pyramids and sphinx, Stonehenge, the Anasazi, the Bimini Road, ancient maps, footprints in prehistoric shale deposits, artifacts found in coal, and many other unexplained objects, constructions, and underwater mysteries are all evidence of a global culture of ancient origin and great longevity—but one that mostly lived in harmony with the earth, leaving us few clues.

So imagine that an immortal race of dynamically healthy people have lived on the earth for a long time, but with strict instructions to not overtly interfere with our civilization. If they have been able to continue learning and growing in knowledge would you be surprised to learn that they had figured out things like electromagnetic propulsion, anti-gravity, and inter-dimensional space travel?

THE ASTRONAUTS

If a human being were born in outer space with extreme low gravity, or zero gravity, would the natural physiological pressures inside the body enlarge the head and eyes? Would the rest of the body suffer from the lack of gravity necessary to build and strengthen bones and muscles? What would that person look like? I find it interesting that reports and accounts of seeing aliens are similar to this image—large head, large eyes.

Go to your computer browser and type in *aliens;* what do you see?—a small, thin creature with bulging head and eyes. The point is not whether the preceding image is an actual alien or not, but rather that so many people all around the world report seeing a similar type and shape of character, a living being we associate with alien visitors and space travel.

How long has this been going on?

Or should we ask, who was it the Nazca people saw in Peru over 2,500 years ago? It seems they saw something flying through the sky—as evidenced by the lines on the ground, but there is also evidence that they saw the beings up close. The Nazca people bound their children's heads to elongate and enlarge them, apparently to mimic the visiting aliens.

Why did the Nazca draw the monumental images on the ground, only seen from high above? I believe they wanted the flying aliens to come back and stay with them permanently. Large-skulled aliens, sharing advanced technology and traveling between dimensions—sounds like *Indiana Jones and the Kingdom of the Crystal Skull* (2008), doesn't it?

I believe the aliens we have seen are us—some of our living ancestors. Immortals. People who have moved from the Garden into outer space and have ships that travel freely between the two dimensions—the two worlds, physical and spiritual, appearing briefly and either shooting away quickly or simply disappearing.

These relatives are able to suffer through the dynamics of their physical changes and space travel, because they get to eat from the Tree of Life, which apparently heals DNA damage, space sickness, and allows their children to change so drastically without dying.

Find someone who really knows about recovered alien bodies and ask them about a haplotype analysis of the space alien mitochondrial DNA (ref. the possible crash in Roswell). I would not be surprised to learn that it is dead on, one hundred percent human—a perfect match to a shared mother—and they cannot explain it.

Apparently, from anecdotal evidence, some of their ships have crashed, which means the United States government does have alien technology—fodder for the science fiction movies and television shows.

Carl Sagan wrote:

It follows that there is the statistical likelihood that Earth was visited by an advanced extraterrestrial civilization at least once during historical times. There are serious difficulties in demonstrating such a contact by ancient writings and iconography alone. Nevertheless, there are *legends* which might profitably be studied in this context.[2]

The Fermi paradox, as developed by physicist Enrico Fermi, states that if our sun is a typical star, and there are billions of stars in the galaxy with Earth-like planets, it is statistically probable that a planet would have life and that life would eventually have interstellar travel and could visit us. If all of this were true, Earth would have had extraterrestrial visitors. If intelligent life is common in the universe, there should be evidence here—besides us.

In a 2013 article, NASA's Kepler mission results suggest that there could be 9.6 to 19.2 *billion* habitable planets just in this galaxy—some as close as thirteen light years away.[3]

Thirteen light years is close enough to make contact, even if only by radio and television transmissions.

And the legends are there.

Throughout history, we find stories and mythology surrounding ancient aliens—possible visitors from other planets in the galaxy. Advanced people visited historical figures in the Bible (ref. Abraham's visit—Genesis 18). People believe the Mayans, Indians, Egyptians, and others had alien visitors, ancient astronauts, or superior elders, who helped them with agriculture, science, and technology. Some Mayan artifacts even look like astronauts and spaceships.

Because of Genesis chapter 1, I would even suggest that we might be the first—the original intelligent species in the universe, or one of the first. We do not "hear" from others, because either they are not there yet, or are not much more advanced. Another hypothesis suggests that it is in the alien's best interest to avoid human contact as much as possible. So what is going on and what is the answer?

There have been aliens, but they are from here—for now. They are our cousins, revealed in the remnants of civilizations buried under the ocean and alluded to in ancient texts, carvings, and geology. They are not extraterrestrials—originating from outside the limits of this solar system, but intra-terrestrials—originating from here—from Earth and the spiritual parallel dimension.

Aliens among us.

SNATCHINGS

As I have pointed out, certain relatives of ours seem to operate in space, in the spiritual realm. We have a spirit, unseen—a part of us, so there is a connection, and maybe it is less tenuous than we think.

Can these "cousins" attack us through the spiritual realm? People make outrageous claims of attacks by creatures in the spiritual realm, and we sweep them away in disgust and abject disbelief. How can they prove an experience like that? What is their defense? It would be wiser and more prudent for the victims to remain silent.

When I heard stories of alien abductions, where a person felt like part of them was taken away by creatures and had something done to them that later showed up in their physical bodies, I thought of our space-faring relatives. If they can move freely through the physical and spiritual dimensions, they could have the ability to manipulate humans from the other side—the spiritual side.

Why would this happen? Did they make a mistake going into space, trying to live there permanently, where it was hard on their bodies and left them deformed and weak? Was the great Tree of Life unable to fix the damage completely, so that only an infusion of DNA from healthy humans could help?

Should angels protect us from them if these cousins are operating outside the rules? We might not be aware of the help: How many other intrusions would have happened except for angelic intervention? Perhaps all we need to do is pray. Simple or simplistic? Yet it seems that the people they seek are those least likely to pray for or expect spiritual help. Alternatively, perhaps, our cousins have a way of working around the restrictions God put in place.

So before you laugh, wiping your eyes at these reports, park your disbelief. Pause a second and wonder if there is something to these accounts of alien spiritual attacks, which all have in common. Because when events like these are unseen, unknown, and for all practical purposes unsubstantiated with scientific evidence and facts, it is easy to be skeptical and dismissive—our default position.

How many people have remained silent when seeing or experiencing something unusual, because they rightly feared the ridicule and rejection we dish out? Something is going on there, and I am not willing to dismiss blithely the claims without further investigation—and prayer.

BIBLICAL EVIDENCE

Does the Bible mention these ancestors of Adam and Eve?

Yes.

The Bible has a specific purpose in mind: the post-Garden account of the descendants of Adam *after* the Great Fall, and only alludes to what happened in the Garden before and after. For the Bible, those previous children of Adam and Eve and the story of their lives— past and present—have no bearing or relevancy on the message or purpose of the Bible— the redemption of humankind after the Fall by God himself.

However, as I said, they are briefly mentioned.

Cain was fearful for his life after he killed Abel, and said, *"Whoever finds me will kill me"* (Gen 4:14). If Cain and Abel are the first children of Adam and Eve outside the Garden, we are talking about only four people—total. So whom is he worried about? Is he afraid one of his parents will clobber him? Certainly not. What people would want to punish him for this premeditated murder?

Cain was worried about his relations, who were born to Eve and elected to live outside the Garden. Premeditated murder was probably unheard of. Cain knew he had crossed a line and imagined a severe and justified punishment. I wonder if a primitive "eye for an eye" law was in effect. That would explain why he was so worried.

Although we know Eve had three boys *after being expelled* (Cain, Abel, Seth—and later on others), now we know where Cain found a wife—among his other family.

If God told my great grandparents, they would have to move from a life of serene contentment into great hardship, I would definitely elect to go with them, as a source of comfort, help, and support.

The Bible does not tell us how much time passed before Adam and Eve had the first two boys, but a well-established culture was thriving by that time. Seasonal sacrifices to God were the norm (Gen 4:3-5); God was physically present at times (Gen 4:9, 14); a system of law, order, and justice was in practice with knowledge of what pleased and displeased God (Gen 4:3); Cain spoke to God as a brassy smart aleck (Gen 4:9, *"Am I my brother's keeper?"* Cain must have been a teenager); sin and the idea of mastering it (Gen 4:7); fear of retribution (Gen 4:14); vengeance (Gen 4:15). The boys were able to find wives (Gen 4:17, 26). We see a complex system in what I assume was a relatively short time, at least compared to how long Adam and Eve had been in the Garden.

Cain's fear of not being in God's presence anymore, *"I will be hidden from your presence"* (Gen 4:14), leads me to believe that even God helped establish Adam and Eve in the formidable land after they were ejected from the Garden.

Adam and Eve did not start to age until expelled from the Garden. It seems Eve had Cain and Abel not long after the ejection, but we cannot know for sure. We do know about when the third child was born.

> When Adam had lived 130 years [outside the Garden], he had a son in his own likeness, in his own image; and he named him Seth. After Seth was born, Adam lived 800 years and had other sons and daughters. Altogether, Adam lived 930 years, and then he died (Gen 5:3-5).

By the time Seth was born, Adam had been outside the Garden for 130 years, and Seth becomes the oldest child at home.

Adam's age is recorded in relation to Seth, not Cain or Abel, because the lineage of Seth is more important, leading to Abraham, which then leads to David and Jesus (Luke 3:23-37—Genealogy of Jesus back to Adam).

We read that eventually Cain moved to the land of Nod, east of Eden (or the entrance to Eden), had a son, and began building a city (Gen 4:17). He *"lay with his wife"* and built a city? Ambitious young man. How many people were there? Apparently, a lot more people than we can imagine, even if the word *village* would have been more precise.

Many families born in the Garden went with Adam and Eve, although some had been living outside the Garden long before the Fall, as shown in archeological and geological discoveries. Further, some children might have eaten of the forbidden tree and the angel forced them from the Garden long before Adam and Eve. But for others, there were no rules—they could come and go freely. *Still do.*

Here is an interesting passage from Genesis 6:

> When men began to increase in numbers on the earth and daughters were born to them, the sons of God saw that the daughters of men were beautiful, and they married any of them they chose. The Nephilim were on the earth in those days—and also afterward—when the sons of God went to the daughters of men and had children by them. They were heroes of old, men of renown (Gen 6:1-2, 4).

Who were these sons of God?

At first reading, it sounds like a compatible but superior race—the Nephilim—decided the daughters of an inferior race—Daughters of Men—pleased them. Different groups fit this description.

Angels

Job 1:6, *"Now there was a day when the sons of God came to present themselves before the LORD, and Satan also came among them."* People love the idea of angels falling in love and then falling from grace, sort of giving up their immortality. Stuff for the movies.

Israelites
In Hosea 1:10, Israelites are the sons of God.

Yet the number of the sons of Israel will be like the sand of the sea, which cannot be measured or numbered; And in the place where it is said to them, "You are not My people,' It will be said to them, 'You are the sons of the living God."

Peacemakers
Matthew 5:9, *"Blessed are the peacemakers, for they shall be called* sons of God."

Believers
"For all who are being led by the Spirit of God, these are the sons of God" (Romans 8:12-25).

Nephilim
Because of a sentence in Jude's short letter, a few people believe the Nephilim were angels. He wrote:

The angels who did not stay within their own position of authority, but left their proper dwelling, he has kept in eternal chains under gloomy darkness until the judgment of the great day (Jude 1:6).

Some have suggested that these fallen angels are the Nephilim (ref. Harper's Bible Dictionary), who desired the daughters of men and intermarried with them. But Jude is not saying that at all. Jude warns his readers to contend for the faith, avoiding sin and evil people. As an admonition, Jude describes the punishment of three groups: people delivered from Egypt in the time of Moses, who did not believe; the angels who abandoned their posts; and the citizens of Sodom and Gomorrah, who did not control their sexual desires.

These three serve as an example of those who suffer the punishment of eternal fire (Jude 1:7).

In army parlance, it sounds like these angels were Absent Without Leave (AWOL), leaving their posts, positions of authority. Did they fall with Satan? These could be some of the angels defeated and captured by Michael and his angelic army, when they fought Satan (Rev 12:7), because Jude says they are in chains until the final judgment. What do you do with captured enemy angels? Most appropriately, lock them up!

However, these sons of God, the Nephilim, were the children of Adam and Eve who came out of the Garden to support them. Hebrew legends say they were a race of "fabulous giants, or semi-divine heroes of a far-remote age of antiquity."[4] This legend is exactly right on. Numbers 13:33 tells us that relatives of the Nephilim, the sons of Anak, were tall people, so that the Israelites felt like grasshoppers around them. The Nephilim were humans. Big by our standards, but people like us.

They gave their daughters to the boys of Adam and Eve, and it appears Adam's boys took daughters from them. Intermarriage.

I believe the Nephilim and Neanderthal were the same or closely related. I have always wondered that the Neanderthal had a larger brain and seemed to be better equipped to live in this world, but apparently disappeared. The human forehead is larger than the Neanderthal, which makes childbirth more difficult *and painful*—part of Eve's punishment.

Then there is the theory that the human race assimilated the Neanderthal people. Genetic evidence points to a sharing of immune system genes, which scientists believe we inherited from them, *or an older group*. I think Adam would qualify as an archaic human of an older genetic source. However, according to the Bible, this sharing is not surprising if a relatively small population of Nephilim already lived outside the Garden or joined Adam and Eve and freely exchanged daughters back and forth with the new post-Fall generation of relatives.

In order to interbreed, the Neanderthal would be giving up their children's immortality—an interesting and tough choice *unless* this group also could not live in the Garden because they ate of the forbidden tree at an earlier time, creating a society on the outside that may have existed for thousands of years before Adam and Eve joined them. Then it would make perfect sense to have their kids marry into Adam and Eve's new family, and it would explain the presence of an active and diverse infrastructure so early in the story of the Fall.

The punishment for Eve was to give birth to a different kind of child: perhaps a child with a larger, differently-shaped head, making childbirth more difficult. A child that would become mostly hairless, have a different take on the world—prone to violence, murder, and pride—with the palpable ability to destroy the planet sustaining them. Where the ancient inhabitants of Earth sought to adapt to the landscape by treading softly, leaving few traces, this new race would seek to transform it into their image. This race of children, with a radically different destiny, would require someone to intervene and save them and the world.

THE

CHAPTER SIXTEEN

UNCHANGED
ONES

When I call these people the Unchanged Ones, I mean they are from the Garden—now, immortal, and well-suited for all climates on our planet—essentially unchanged: Some of them will even remember Adam and Eve. They venture in and out of our world, the way we go from the kitchen to the living room, foraging, exploring the high and lonesome places, causing great excitement and wonder when glimpsed, or their presence suspected.

In our world, where even the most elusive and mysterious snow leopard has been found and studied extensively, why can't we find this creature? Because this being is smart—scary smart. It sees or senses the trail cameras, the long-range photographer on a distant ridge, and the patient watchers.

There is an elusive creature known on every continent, yet has not been captured—dead or alive—and has not been well photographed. In the Himalayas, they call it the Yeti; the Native Americans called it Sasquatch and Big Man. In modern America, we refer to it as Bigfoot.

The Native American community knew about this creature long before the first European explorers landed on their shores. They regarded this personage with great respect, and many thought it was a supernatural spirit being. The Lakota referred to it as Big Man, *both spirit and real being.*

Interestingly, "Ray Owen, son of a Dakota spiritual leader from Prairie Island Reservation in Minnesota said, 'They exist in another dimension from us, but can appear in this dimension whenever they have a reason to. The Big Man come from God. He's our big brother, kind of looks out for us.'"[1]

Now you see how this creature begins to fit into the story. Like their space-faring cousins, these beings watch and wait, making their presence known at different times, while leaving us with more wonder and more questions than answers.

A DESCRIPTION *of a wonderful large WILD MAN, or monſtrous GIANT,*
BROUGHT FROM BOTANY-BAY.

Woodcut, 1789. The Rover crew under Captain Lee captured a nine-foot, seven-inch man, at Botany Bay, who apparently had been living in a cave with others of his kind, transporting him to Plymouth, England.

And that is why there is so little evidence—no true fossil record. They do not typically stay here—in our world. There is no camp or community where they dwell. Mostly, they just visit, although some Native American legends speak of some living in remote areas over extended periods, and a group might have lived at Botany Bay, Australia. You will not find a dead one, or bones, or fossils, because they do not die of what we would consider natural causes. If one is injured or dies in an accident, their friends carry them home—to the Garden, if at all possible. Hunters, who claim to have shot a Bigfoot, say that others came and carried the body off. So the most we will find are footprints—and hair.

We do find hair and that is important.

The Sasquatch Genome Project studied hair samples with follicles—skin and blood—found on fences, trees, other objects and one sample from a deliberate shooting. Criminal forensic scientists, performing examinations through double-blind studies, determined that the creature was a human hybrid.

Based on the results, the new scientific name for Sasquatch is Homo Sapiens Cognatus. "Cognatus" means *related to mother by blood*, because all evidence suggests that Sasquatch is a near relative. How near? The haplotype analysis of the mitochondrial DNA found in the samples, which traces the mother's lineage, was one hundred percent human.

Sasquatch is us!

Right now hunters shoot at Sasquatch on sight. In 2013, Dean Cain and Spike TV posted a $10 million reward for irrefutable evidence of Bigfoot—a bounty—dead or alive.[2] And a senseless tragedy.

A tragedy for two reasons:

1. They are not animals to be shot for sport or money. Like Adam's son, Cain, we kill first and think later. We were all outraged when Cecil the Lion was mortally wounded with an arrow, then shot forty hours later, so he could be skinned for his head and hide (July 2015). Is that what we want to do—kill and butcher our blood relatives? Legislators must pass international and national laws, criminalizing the shooting of this ancient and harmless being. Prison time is required, not a reward.

2. If we could actually sit down with them, we might learn something from our Big Brother. Do you think a person who has successfully lived on this planet for a million plus years could teach us anything? A creature reported to have helped the Native Americans in times of need?

How would that happen? How could we facilitate this meeting—a discussion with Big Brother?

The first challenge: We would have to humble ourselves—no easy task, adjusting our attitude to receive information and not make demands. Then we would need to set up a meeting place centered on the location of multiple hair samples that was non-threatening and simple—not high tech. We would have to present a peace offering, perhaps fruit, vegetables, and nuts—whether eaten by the Visitor or not. Then wait, because I am sure they have the ability to watch and listen without being seen. The Visitors will come when they are sure no possible sign of danger exists, probably at night—at first.

The second step is to say, "I see you," with no further demands: simple recognition without either side requiring more from the other. I would also suggest that our representatives be Native Americans, perhaps Lakota, who already have a long history with these beings, and know the old sign language, which the Sasquatch must have been able to communicate with at one time.

Does this mean that Adam and Eve were like present-day Sasquatch? No, but I think they were bigger and had more hair. Some will reject this idea out of hand, because when we think of Adam and Eve in the Garden, we automatically input the image of ourselves, so we can comprehend the idea, visualize the situation.

Artwork typically shows a naked white-skinned Adam and equally naked Eve with something covering up their sexual parts—all very proper and trim.

Adam and Eve by Lucas Cranach the Elder (1472–1553). *Courtesy the Courtauld Institute Art Gallery, London.*

How hairy were Adam and Eve? They could have been as hairy as a goat. Why would I say that, tarnishing our artistic image and delusion? Because many of the earliest post-Fall grandchildren of Adam and Eve were also quite hairy, as are some even today.

In Genesis 25, Esau is born covered in red hair: "Esau" means *hairy*. Then, in Genesis 27, we learn that Isaac is old and mostly blind. He wants to bless his firstborn son, Esau, so he sends him into the field to hunt wild game for a special meal, which he loves. Isaac's wife, Rebecca, hears this and prepares her second-born son, Jacob, to steal the blessing meant for Esau.

Jacob is worried. *"My brother Esau is a hairy man, and I am a man with smooth skin. What if my father touches me? I would appear to be tricking him and would bring down a curse on myself rather than a blessing"* (Gen 27:11-12). But Rebecca has figured everything out. *"She also covered his hands and the smooth part of his neck with goatskins"* (verse 16).

The goatskins covering Jacob fooled Isaac, and Jacob received the blessing meant for Esau, who did not really care about it (Gen 27:28-29). At a later time, God changed Jacob's name to Israel (Gen 32:28).

Goats are covered in hair, and all through the ages, there have been people almost as hairy, those not suffering from a genetic disease. Just incredibly hairy people.

Adam and Eve were one with their environment—naked and not ashamed (Gen 2:25). It makes sense that they would have some layer of hair to protect them from the environment. Even in a place as perfect as Eden, they would experience some temperature fluctuations, the cool of night, and rain.

In our own world, over a relatively short time, people have diverged in color, shape, and size. In Africa, the Hamitic Sudanese and Watutsi of Rwanda are extremely tall, while the Baka and Mbenga pygmies are extremely short.

Pygmies.

Since the time Adam and Eve left the Garden, all around the world, people come in all different shapes, sizes, and colors. So can you imagine some slight to major differences in our cousins after millions of years?

I have explained how the people moving into outer space could have changed due to environmental factors—larger head and eyes, diminutive bodies. Some of these forest people, Sasquatch, could have trended toward a greater size and strength, as they continued in the food gathering society God originally created. Immortal. Wise. Some might have known Adam and Eve personally, and could tell amazing stories. At times, they helped the Native Americans and others around the world. Closely related. Aliens among us.

And in our natural arrogance, we place a bounty on them.

Our cousins from the Garden—on the ground and in the air—do not play a part in our history, except where I mentioned the earliest sharing of mates, and perhaps in some snatching incidents. Otherwise, I am sure someone told them to let our story unfold naturally, without interference. Why? Because everyone wants Satan defeated in the end—them and us.

CHAPTER SEVENTEEN
CHOICES

We have talked a lot about aliens and their actual and possible roles in our lives and future. You may or may not buy into all I have mentioned, but I hope the arguments and examples are compelling and get you thinking. There is a war. And I hope you are interested enough to ask the question, "Which side do I want to be on?"

All other ideas aside, if Jesus does indeed come back *before* 2037 as he foretold—before this generation passes away—and he takes to him only those people who believe in him, what should you do?

I think of belief in Jesus as having a boarding pass for the New Jerusalem starship. It is more than that, of course, but you get the idea. That is certainly a benefit for believers.

The Apostle Paul tells us in his letter to the Romans that those people who do not get the opportunity to choose a side (don't hear the Good News) will be judged by God based on their actions (Romans 1:20, 2:13–16). However, for those who hear about the world's alien visitor, Jesus, there are three choices: Jesus, Not Jesus, Wait.

Choosing Jesus is self-explanatory, and I will talk more about that in a minute.

I gave you the Not Jesus option, because it was less dramatic than saying you could choose *Satan's Side*, and less ambiguous than choosing *The Ways of the World*. The idea is that you can choose Jesus or not. Rejecting or ignoring the Jesus option gives you the same outcome. It means you do not buy into what I have said, or you do not feel compelled to make a decision. Or a hybrid of the two, where you sort of wonder about Jesus and the ideas of the book, perhaps worry a little, but you like things the way they are—status quo. "I like what you wrote, but don't rock my boat, or ask me to get into a different boat—at least not right now."

Waiting

Some of you are going to wait and see if any of the things I've predicted come true—a short, temporary war in the Middle East that allows Israel to rebuild the Great Temple; a leader who miraculously survives an assassination attempt; fire falling from heaven at someone's command and a great statue coming to life; a world war. Then you might make a choice. The problem with waiting or procrastinating is that you might die while doing so. Do not let that happen, gambling with your eternal life.

Some of you might belong to another religion, or you might have questions about Jesus: who he is and what this is all about. You might be concerned that some followers of Jesus have done terrible things over the centuries. You might have questions about specific issues and possible conflicts in the Bible. Did God create evil? Does God allow wicked people to prosper, unpunished, and good people to suffer, sometimes without ever seeing justice? Does he ever intervene?

Many people, believers and unbelievers, love Jesus but do not care for the Church, which might mean people in the Church have been frightfully brutal and hurtful at times, to you specifically, or in general. Others don't care for the Church, because it asks for money and tells people how to live their lives. All of these are good thoughts and questions, and I encourage you to explore them.

However, make the choice, now, then explore.

You can always change your mind and walk away—sad but true. It is often a heart-mind conflict. You can tell God you have concerns (mind), but you still want to express faith and hope in him (heart). And expressing belief in Jesus does not mean you have to believe everything I've speculated on in this book.

Rational non-belief

Then there are people who wonder if God exists at all, or how it might be possible for us to know him. I know people who want empirical evidence of God, not based on or requiring faith. They tell me that not even a visit by God in a vision or dream would suffice them, because it could not be trusted, and they would not trust their own eyes. That if they see someone healed, even themselves, they would remain skeptical. The Bible talks about this dilemma.

The Apostle Paul addressed a similar issue in his first letter to the Corinthian church.

The Message that points to Christ on the cross seems like sheer silliness to those hellbent on destruction, but for those on the way of salvation it makes perfect sense. This is the way God works, and most powerfully as it turns out. It's written, "I'll turn conventional wisdom on its head, I'll expose so-called experts as crackpots." So where can you find someone truly wise, truly educated, truly intelligent in this day and age? Hasn't God exposed it all as pretentious nonsense? Since the world in all its fancy wisdom never had a clue when it came to knowing God, God in his wisdom took delight in using what the world considered dumb—preaching, of all things!—to bring those who trust him into the way of salvation (1 Cor 1:18-25, The Message translation).

What this means is that if a person persists in their rational disbelief, not willing to take God on faith, they will probably die that way: "I will only believe if God meets this or that criteria." Could it be that this person is suffering from a delusion, by one who is feeding them lies?

The god of this age has blinded the minds of unbelievers, so that they cannot see the Light of the Gospel of the glory of Christ, who is the image of God (2 Cor 4:4).

What a pathetic tragedy.

Another aspect of this "blinding" is how we have lived. Many people do not have a church background and have not grown up with a conscious understanding or concept of God. If they even think about God, he is often judged and questioned by their experience in the world and misconception about who and what he is. Is he Santa Claus, handing out favors and extra helpings to good little boys and girls? Or a genie, granting wishes to those who are lucky or desperate enough? If we have a tough or wretched time in our life, then God seems remote or non-existent—even irrelevant. When he does not meet our needs as expected, we accuse him of being unfaithful. We must blame someone, and God is a big target.

A gentleman once told me (and on another occasion, a lady) that God could not forgive him because he had done so many wicked things—he did not deserve it. More Santa Claus thinking, that we must be good little kids to get presents and favors. The problem is you can never be good enough to win or earn God's approval. God understands: The idea behind GRACE is that *you do not deserve it.* And Jesus said you were exactly the kind of person he came to save and to help:

> *It is not the healthy who need a doctor, but the sick. I have not come to call the righteous, but sinners to repentance* (Luke 5:31-32). *For the Son of Man came to seek and to save the lost* (Luke 19:10).

I talked earlier about how our present situation on Earth—pain and suffering—was our choice, our decision, based on Adam and Eve's disobedience in the Garden. The results of the Fall changed how we understood and knew God. The people living in the Garden easily knew all of these questions. God was there, walking with them in the cool of the evening. "Hey God, how do crickets make that sound?" He reaches down, smiling, and the little cricket jumps into his hand. Pointing to the legs, he explains how . . .

One purpose in the coming of the Messiah to Earth was to show us how to re-establish that broken connection, broken relationship. The Kingdom of Heaven on Earth, as Jesus described it, could be a type and shadow of life in heaven, while still living here (Matt 18:1-3). Yes, we can learn to hear God's voice in our lives, to come to an understanding of our purpose here on Earth, and experience transformation in our hearts and minds.

So I encourage people with questions to hold onto them and learn the answers.

I have shown that we are at war and by default perishing. Jesus said it was something we needed to be saved from. Saved. The Baptist church did not invent the idea of salvation. Jesus said it first, appealing to the story of the snake on a pole during the time of Moses (Num 21:8-9), and then explaining that this image was pointing to himself.

> *Just as Moses lifted up the snake in the wilderness, so the Son of Man must be lifted up,* (crucified) *that everyone who believes in him may have eternal life* (John 3:14–15).

When people bitten by the poisonous snakes looked to the bronze snake on the staff, they were healed. Two verses later, Jesus explains why:

> *For God so loved the world that he gave his one and only Son, that whoever believes in him shall not perish but have eternal life. For God did not send his Son into the world to condemn the world, but to save the world through him* (John 3:16-17).

Save the world. The world is at war, and God's intent was to enter it, saving as many people as he could.

If the world is a sinking ship, God has thrown a lifeboat into the water, rowing around, calling out, while pulling everyone into the boat who reaches out to him. We could even say that God gets in the water, giving up his seat to be sure everyone can find a place. In that respect, this book is part of that analogy—calling out, explaining the situation, and imploring people to get on board—not just the boat but the great starship, which is not an analogy at all.

WARNING

Jesus said that if you chose him:

You will be hated by everyone because of me, but the one who stands firm to the end will be saved (Matt 10:22).

We are saved by God's amazing grace, but there is a sense in the scriptures, that after we choose God, we assure our seat on the ship by being good, helpful to others, and faithful until the day we die or are taken to the presence of Jesus.

In other words, this choice comes with an admonition: If you chose God's side, the World—its system and values—will hate you. Why? *Because we are at war and you are changing sides!* You are choosing to oppose Satan's way of things. So to choose Jesus instead, you will be in conflict with the World, which means the World's emphasis on pride, control, elevation of self before or above others, and direction.

Direction? Absolutely. God started it when he said, *"I, even I am the LORD, and apart from me there is no savior"* (Isaiah 43:11).

Jesus continued the family tradition when he said, *"I am the Way, the Truth, and the Life. No one can come to the Father except through me"* (John 14:6 NLT, also Matt 7:13-14).

These statements have floored people for centuries. Many of you reading this book have agreed with me on every aspect, no matter how outrageous—until now. Audacious and exclusive. Some will say, "How dare Jesus speak that way when the World believes there are many valid beliefs and paths to the Divine?" Some people will announce that if that is the way it is—Jesus or nothing—then they will not believe in Jesus. Has the god of this age blinded them, or what?

Isn't that what I have been talking about?

If you reject the Jesus Way—which God and Jesus both say is the only way, you are saying you want to get on the New Jerusalem *your own way*—sort of create your own ticket—or you will decide to reject the whole thing. Little gods. "My way! My way! Don't tell me what to do, and by all means don't tell me how to do it!" Really?

Tell someone that the only way to board the New Jerusalem is to believe in Jesus, and see what their reaction is. The World shouts, loudly and repeatedly, that there are many ways to God—not one. So by choosing Jesus, you will instantly be in the minority. In some cases, your life might even be in danger (especially the Middle East, parts of India, parts of Africa—see *Persecution.com* for a comprehensive listing).

Jesus prayed to God for us, and it follows what I've been telling you:

I have given them (believers) *your Word and the World has hated them,* (the World is opposed, by default, to the things of God) *for they are not of the World any more than I am of the World* (and what did the World do to Jesus?). *My prayer is not that you take them out of the World but that you protect them from the Evil One* (Satan, the devil, the dragon, and his many agents) (John 17:14-15).

One theme in this book is that two alien groups are at war, constantly fighting. We are in the middle and have the ability to know that one group represents good and the other opposes it. The good side sent a representative to live among us, whose short life and statements changed the world, while announcing a way to choose his side. That by choosing his message and believing in him as The Messenger, we will move into his spiritual realm when our body dies and experience a better life while still here. When I say "better," I am not promoting prosperity, but quality.

If the arguments I have presented are compelling and you are brave enough to make the decision; if you want to choose Jesus, rejecting the Prince of this World and his system and values, all you have to do is tell God you are ready. Say this:

> Dear God, forgive me. Save me. I choose Jesus. I choose the side of Good and Love; guide me in how to live that way. I want to go to heaven and be on that great ship with you. I want to be on the winning side. Amen.

Add more to this prayer if you want to.

I know this prayer is simple, but not simplistic. Rather, it expresses where your heart is. God sees into your heart. By few words or many, or whether they are said a certain way, covering all of the dogmatic points, they are not as important as the choice you have made, with sincerity.

> *I the LORD search the heart and examine the mind, to reward each person according to their conduct, according to what their deeds deserve* (Jer 17:10).

GOOD WORKS

We do not gain God's favor or win our way into heaven by good works. We are saved *only by God's grace*, through confessed belief in the work of Jesus—his life and resurrection. Why? Because God hates pride, and if we could work our way into his good graces, then we could boast: I got to heaven without you!

> *For it is by grace you have been saved, through faith—and this not from yourselves, it is the gift of God—not by works, so that no one can boast* (Eph 2:8-9).

However, after you are saved, good works are expected, as your life reflects a change in what God is doing inside you.

The idea is that if you prayed for God to save you, your life will change—from the inside out, while we are encouraged to turn willfully and purposefully from a life of self-centeredness to other-centeredness—thinking of others before ourselves.

C. S. Lewis wrote: "Repentance means unlearning all the self-conceit and self-will that we have been training ourselves into."[1]

If you did not pray and do not intend to, at least I hope you enjoyed the read and don't feel like you've wasted your time. But if you just prayed sincerely and chose Jesus, I want to thank you for your courage and humility.

Now, as a new believer, please do three things:

1. Learn and pray. Start reading the New Testament Gospels—Matthew, Mark, Luke, John. Gospel means *Good News*. Focus on the Gospels for now. Do what Jesus asks you to do there; he prizes obedience. Most churches will give you a Bible, if you do not have one. I use the New International Version, but I also really like the New American Standard.

Read the Psalms, as I mentioned before. The Psalms will reveal the heart of God and teach you to pray and hear his voice in your life. Prayer is simply you talking to God. Practice and learn it. I told you the Psalms are a great guide in this area, but think of prayer as a conversation. I smile to remember Tevye in *Fiddler on the Roof*, looking up while pulling his milk wagon, and talking to God like a friend, sharing his problems and concerns. And so it is. Be honest, be frank, and share your heart. Then be quiet. Because in time, you will learn to hear the voice of God: *it is a conversation after all*, and he is easier to hear if you are not talking all the time. Also because God seldom shouts; he whispers. *"And after the earthquake there was a fire, but the LORD was not in the fire. And after the fire there was the sound of a gentle whisper"* (1 Kings 19:12).

2. As a new warrior on the side of Good, you fight and beat the enemy by treating people right—treating them good. You know what right is, because you know when people treat you right. You have all heard of the Golden Rule. As Jesus concluded the Sermon on the Mount, he said, *"In everything, do to others what you would have them do to you"* (Matt 7:12, 22:36-40). We all want to be treated with respect. So take the initiative and be nice—be good and gracious because you want to be treated the same way. Being gracious means you are nice to people who do not necessarily deserve it; that you take the high road in a situation or relation, not seeking vengeance or falling into criticism and anger or hate.

So simply be nice to others. Be kind. Be helpful. Be an encourager. If you do not feel like this is particularly in your nature, do not give up, keep trying and your nature will change—with God's help. I know it is a small part, but every effort is important and shows you have changed sides in this ancient conflict.

God values sacrificial love. He is sacrificial love and pure humility, so he rejects the proud and pretentious, who are haughty, condescending, and arrogant (Gal 5:13-26)—those who are judgmental and critical. He chooses the weak and insignificant (1 Cor 1:27-31). That is why he tells us to humble ourselves, and love others as much as we obviously love ourselves (Matt 22:39;

John 13:34-35). That is why he says the meek will inherit the earth (Matt 5:5). It's hard. Pride, and the intense focus on self—my needs, my interests, my wants, my desires . . . has been the human race's default position since the Fall. Some of us do not know anything else.

3. Attend a church that studies the Bible, teaches from the pulpit how to live the Gospel, and believes Jesus will return soon. Find one and faithfully go every time the doors are open.

Why attend church? Think of church as a support group of like-minded individuals. In the community called Church, you should be learning how to follow Jesus in this great struggle, putting into practice what he tells us to do in the Gospels (helping and encouraging each other to grow spiritually, Heb 10:24-25). Imperfectly at first, I know, but with increasing success as it becomes a habit.

If they have small groups, join one and attend faithfully. At church, you learn the big picture of things, but in the small group, you learn to apply them and are held accountable. *"Those who walk with the wise grow wise"* (Proverbs 13:20).

Theology is the study of God. When we study our Bibles, the result can be all head knowledge, or through obedience to what we read, can produce a life shaped by the story, words, and sacrifice of Jesus Christ. When we experience inner change and transformation, our lives can have a positive impact on the world. Shouldn't this be particularly true now? I mean, in these End Times, as the darkness spreads and deepens, a candle shines brighter, and a candelabra lights up the world.

Your decision to believe in Jesus does not mean you have to vote Republican or join the Conservative Coalition. How you vote and what you believe about other matters is for you alone. What is important is that you have joined the winning side. Do not waiver when times get tough in the future, which they surely will. Jesus told us that life on this planet would get unbearably hard just before he returns. That is another reason why joining a church can be helpful (Matt 24, Luke 21)—mutual support.

In the military, we send new recruits to basic training. In that course of instruction, soldiers learn the history of war, the latest in ongoing conflicts, how to act appropriately, how to fight, and how to work together. So it is in the church. As I explained, there is a war going on. We learn the basics of our faith by attending church and studying our Bible; we learn to live and work together by attending church, bible studies, and small groups; and in these places, we learn to be effective soldiers in the ongoing fight.

In combat, when the bullets start flying, you don't run away, because you are obedient and focused on a goal, but also because you want to support your friends and be supported by them. If you do not really want to do the "church" part, please reconsider. Find one you like, meeting the criteria above, and faithfully stick with it. Sadly, humans have the ability to mess up good things—like church—so be patient and take that into account. Be gracious.

Expect Satan to whisper in your ear, suggesting that church is not necessary, because if he can isolate you from other believers, you could be in danger of going back into your old ways, essentially giving up your boarding pass. It would be like talking a soldier into deserting during a time of war—a grave mistake.

The Apostle Paul warned:

Let us not become weary in doing good, for at the proper time we will reap a harvest if we do not give up (Gal 6:9).

And Jesus said the same thing:

I am coming soon. Hold fast what you have, so that no one may seize your crown (Rev 3:11).

The best way to sum up what I have written here is to reaffirm that everything is contingent on the return of Jesus, with signs to watch for as the time draws near. And he is the one who issues the boarding passes for the New Jerusalem.

Jesus said:

Behold, I am coming soon! My reward is with me, and I will give to everyone according to what they have done (Rev 22:12).

If you found this book interesting, and if you believe people should choose Jesus so they can be on the winning side and board the New Jerusalem, please share this book with others.

ENDNOTES

Chapter 1

1. Naifei Zhan, et al. "From Brittle to Ductile: A Structure Dependent Ductility of Diamond Nanothread," arXiv - Cornell University Library (Nov 2015): http://arxiv.org/ftp/arxiv/papers/1511/1511.01583.pdf.
2. Sheila A. Thibeault, et al. "Radiation Shielding Materials Containing Hydrogen, Boron, and Nitrogen: Systematic Computational and Experimental," NAIC Presentation v8b (March 2012): http://www.nasa.gov/pdf/638828main_Thibeault_Presentation.pdf.
3. John Ira Petty, page editor, "The Right Stuff for Super Spaceships" (16 September 2002): http://www.nasa.gov/vision/space/gettingtospace/16sep_rightstuff.html.

Chapter 4

1. Tuomo Suntola, "The Dynamic Universe—space as a spherical closed energy system," *International Journal of Astrophysics and Space Science* 2, no. 6-1 (2014): 66–85.
2. Steven Weinberg, *The First Three Minutes—A Modern View of the Origin of the Universe* (New York: Basic Books, 1977), 154—winner of the Nobel Prize in Physics 1979.
3. St. Athanasius of Alexandria 296–373AD, *The Incarnation and the Word of God*, 3:12.
4. Adam Frank, "3 Theories That Might Blow Up the Big Bang," DiscoverMagazine.com (April 2008): http://discovermagazine.com/2008/apr/25-3-theories-that-might-blow-up-the-big-bang.

Chapter 5

1. Stuart Clark, "Alien megastructure could explain mysterious new Kepler results," TheGuardian.com (Oct 2015): www.theguardian.com/science/across-the-universe/2015/oct/16/alien-megastructure-could-explain-mysterious-new-kepler-results.

Chapter 7

1. James J. Gettel, *God's Love, Human Freedom, & Christian Faith,* (St. Louis, Missouri: Chalice Press 2003), 11–12 (based on the *Parable of the King and the Maiden* by Søren Kierkegaard in *Philosophical Fragments*, 1844, with some Kierkegaard direct quotes).

Chapter 8

1. Daniel Zohary and Maria Hopf, *Domestication of Plants in the Old World*, 3th ed. (Oxford, UK: University Press, 2000).
2. Carl Zimmer, "Agriculture Linked to DNA Changes in Ancient Europe," *New York Times* online (23 Nov 2015): www.nytimes.com/2015/11/24/science/agriculture-linked-to-dna-changes-in-ancient-europe.html?_r=0.
3. Ibid., Zimmer.
4. Ibid., Zimmer.

Chapter 9

1. A. Frank and W. T. Sullivan III, "A New Empirical Constraint on the Prevalence of Technological Species in the Universe," *Astrobiology* 16, no. 5 (2016): 1-5.

Chapter 10

1. C. S. Lewis Pte Ltd, *Mere Christianity* (New York, NY: HarperCollins, 1952), 121.
2. "Jesus Brother of Satan," www.mormonvoices.org/1/jesus-brother-of-satan, (19 July 2011).

Chapter 11

1. Franz Werfel, *The Song of Bernadette* (New York: Viking Press, 1942), 186.
2. Ibid., Werfel, 206.
3. Ibid., Werfel, 154.
4. Ibid., Werfel, 299.

Chapter 14

1. Donald Johanson and Maitland Edey, *Lucy—The Beginnings of Humankind: How our oldest human ancestor was discovered – and who she was* (New York: Touchstone, 1981), 20.
2. Charles Darwin, *The Origin of the Species: By Means of Natural Selection*, 6th ed. (London: Murray, 1872) 306–308.
3. Maddie Stone, "This microbial animal threw the evolutionary rulebook out the window," Gizmodo.com (Nov 2015): http://gizmodo.com/this-microbial-animal-threw-the-evolutionary-rulebook-0-1743035057.
4. e.g., "Darwin, *The Origin of the Species*, 167."
5. Charles Darwin and Sir Francis Darwin, *The Life and Letters of Charles Darwin* (London: Murray, 1887), 304.

6. Ulrich Hildebrand, "Das Universum – Hinweis auf Gott?" Ethos – die Zeitschrift für die ganze Familie, No. 10 (Oct 1988), 16:59.

7. Brian Thomas, "Dinosaur Fossil Wasn't Supposed to Be There," (14 April 2011): www.icr.org/article/dinosaur-fossil-wasnt-supposed-be-there/.

8. Don Batten, "Living Fossils: a powerful argument for creation," Creation 33, no. 2: (April 2011), 22. Emphasis author.

9. Albert Einstein, *The World as I See It*. Translated by Alan Harris as Mein Weltbild (New Jersey: The Citadel Press, 1999), 29. Originally published by New York: The Wisdom Library.

10. Hans C. Ohanian, *Einstein's Mistakes: The Human Failings of Genius* (New York: W. W. Norton & Co., 2008), 3.

Chapter 15

1. Robin McKie, "When Antarctica was a Tropical Paradise" TheGuardian.com (16 July 2011): www.theguardian.com/world/2011/jul/17/antarctica-tropical-climate-co2-research.

2. Carl Sagan, "Direct Contact among Galactic Civilizations by Relativistic Interstellar spaceflight" SpaceDirect.com and Elsevier Ltd, 11:5 (May 1963): www.sciencedirect.com/science/article/pii/0032063363900722. Emphasis mine.

3. Pete Spotts, "Earth-like Planets Next Door? Prospect could point to 9.6 billion more" The Christian Science Monitor (6 Feb 2013): www.csmonitor.com/USA/2013/0206/Earth-like-planets-next-door-Prospect-could-point-to-9.6-billion-more.

4. Herbert Edward Ryle, *Cambridge Bible for Schools and Colleges* (Cambridge: University Press, 1921), Genesis 6:1–4 commentary.

Chapter 16

1. Jeff Meldrum, *Sasquatch: Legend Meets Science* (New York: Forge Books, 2007), 83.

2. Lee Speigel, "$10 Million Bounty Put On Bigfoot's Hairy Head" Huffington Post. (23 January 2014): www.huffingtonpost.com/2014/01/10/bigfoot-hunters-compete-10-million-dollar-bounty_n_4557209.html.

Chapter 17

1. C. S. Lewis, *Mere Christianity*, 60

THE REV. DR. JOEL CURTIS GRAVES is an Anglican priest in the Anglican Church in North America (ACNA). He tackles some of the Bible's hardest questions and shares ideas about ancient alien factions and how/why things have happened in the Bible from Genesis to Revelation. Joel has been theologically minded since a youth and attended Trinity School for Ministry in Ambridge, Pennsylvania. After a long break, he finished seminary at Faith Evangelical Lutheran Seminary, Tacoma, Washington, where he earned his Master of Divinity and Doctor of Ministry in Leadership. He served as a hospital and hospice chaplain before starting an Anglican church in Lacey, Washington, from which he retired in 2012. He has been married to Rena for more than 40 years, and loves to paint, read, write, golf, go to the movies, spoil the grandkids, and travel.

VISIT HIM AT HIS WEBSITE:
www.AliensGodBible.com.
Facebook: AliensGodBible.